RAGS *to* RUGS

TOM KNISELY

STACKPOLE BOOKS

Essex, Connecticut
Blue Ridge Summit, Pennsylvania

STACKPOLE BOOKS

An imprint of Globe Pequot, the trade division of The Rowman & Littlefield Publishing Group, Inc.
4501 Forbes Blvd., Ste. 200
Lanham, MD 20706
www.rowman.com

Distributed by NATIONAL BOOK NETWORK
800-462-6420

British Library Cataloguing in Publication Information available

Library of Congress Cataloging-in-Publication Data available

ISBN 978-0-8117-7057-6 (paper : alk. paper)
ISBN 978-0-8117-7058-3 (electronic)

♾™ The paper used in this publication meets the minimum requirements of American National Standard for Information Sciences—Permanence of Paper for Printed Library Materials, ANSI/NISO Z39.48-1992.

First Edition

I dedicate this book to my grandsons, Jai and Bodhi. These two little boys offer me a constant source of inspiration for new rugs from their outgrown T-shirts. There is nothing more satisfying than to see them sharing a spot on one of Gumpah's rugs for a little reading time with a favorite book.

When they look down at their rug, the boys recognize some of their old shirts from when they were smaller. They're big boys now. They can read. Everything is just the way it's supposed to be.

CONTENTS

INTRODUCTION

Hello.

If the title of this book has sparked your interest, I feel like I already know a lot about you. I believe we must have some things in common. You hate the idea of being wasteful. Doesn't it hurt your heart to think about all the things that are discarded and thrown into the garbage and landfills? I know it does mine. It's only been in recent years that my rural community has embraced the idea of recycling paper, bottles, and cans. I remember that our family had a burn barrel in the backyard that we used to get rid of much of our noncompostable waste. Paper, cardboard, and sometimes plastics would be placed in the barrel and set on fire to get rid of them. It's horrifying now that I think of it—black smoke from the burning plastics going up into our atmosphere. Clothing was often dropped off at Goodwill or church, but items that they wouldn't take ended up in that burn barrel.

The idea of Reduce, Reuse, and Recycle is not a new concept. People living through lean times have perfected the idea of living very frugally. Certainly, quilters must be recognized for their ingenuity in taking little pieces of perfectly good fabric and reusing them by sewing the fabric pieces into a patterned design. Rag rug weavers wove narrowly cut cloth strips into plain and color patterned warps to make durable floor coverings. Not only did these rag rugs brighten the appearance of a room, but they also helped to keep the floors warmer by blocking out drafts. Families would take their worn and unwanted household textiles and clothing and cut them into narrow strips. Because the strip lengths were often short, women in the family would sit and sew the strips together by hand to make a long and continuous length to make it easier for the weaver to work with. Many times, a conscious effort was made to mix colors in a pleasing arrangement—and sometimes not. When a long length of rags was sewn together, it would be wound into balls. These fabric strip balls were then taken to a weaver, who would weave them into carpeting. The carpets could be woven shorter in the form of scatter rugs, or the weaver might weave long lengths of carpeting for use as a hall runner or stair runners.

I have made a profession of weaving or teaching others to weave for forty-plus years. I have woven many different types of textiles over those years, but my passion is weaving rugs. I especially like weaving rag rugs. For me, the idea of repurposing worn-out fabrics that have lost usefulness for their original purpose into a rug is very satisfying. I think it's like giving these worn and humble fabrics a chance at a new lease on life.

I know you might think that this idea is a little corny and silly, but when I look at a rug and recognize the different bits of fabric, and then remember what they were and where they came from, it tells a story. Take, for instance, weaving a rug for your high school senior's bedroom. The rug could be woven from their pajamas from when they were a toddler. How cool would that be? Another nice memory rug would be one that is woven with the cut strips of fabric from a friend or family member's clothing. I remember a friend telling me that she was going to weave a rag rug using her husband's ties. During his career, he had worn a tie to work every day. To celebrate his retirement, she took dozens of ties from his closet and wove them into a rag rug. I thought it was a wonderful way to close that chapter in his life.

In my previous book, *Weaving Rag Rugs*, I concentrated on the preparation of getting started on your first rag rug. I discussed what looms are best to use to weave a strong, durable rug. I gave suggestions on the proper materials to warp the loom and offered tips on the preparation of the fabric strips. Since you may find this information useful if you don't own that book, I've included a condensed version of it toward the back of this book (see "Rug Weaving Basics" beginning on page 99). In that book, I

also included many pattern ideas and drafts for weaving attractive rag rugs using *new* fabric. Some weavers find it easier to buy and use new and color-coordinated fabrics to decorate a room. When the bedspread, drapes, and rag rugs match, it makes the owner very happy. It's also much easier to buy an eight- or ten-yard bolt of new fabric to prepare nice long strips of weft materials.

For many weavers, the idea of sewing short lengths of fabric harvested from old clothes seems like a daunting task. Rest assured, there are plenty of sources of rag material that can give you long lengths of rags so that the weaving goes quickly and more easily—materials that are inexpensive or even *free*. You can start by asking your family and friends to save their old unwanted jeans, clothes, and sheets. Another good option is to send a shout-out to the websites Nextdoor.com and Freecycle.org. You never can tell what fabulous items are being given away for free. It gives you a nice warm feeling knowing that you are recycling these fabrics and repurposing them into a sturdy rag rug.

With this book, *Rags to Rugs*, it is my intention to show you that you can weave fabulous rugs from unwanted and discarded materials. As you flip through the pages, read about the materials used and ideas behind each rug. I hope you find inspiration for weaving your own rugs using fabrics that might otherwise end up in the trash can and then in a landfill. I have given you suggestions for making rugs woven from old sheets, blankets, unwanted cotton and wool fabrics, factory waste, and even plastic shopping bags. There are also examples of rugs woven from the typically discarded loom waste known as thrums.

As you page through this book, let your mind go wild. Allow my rug patterns to inspire you to create your own terrific rugs and know that you are doing a good thing by reducing waste. Now look at you. Pat yourself on the back for this gallant effort. You're a soldier in the fight to reduce, reuse, and recycle. Way to go!

Happy weaving,
Tom Knisely

BEFORE YOU GET STARTED

I want to give you a few thoughts before you jump ahead and start winding your warp. This is a rag rug book written with an emphasis on using recycled materials, materials that might be considered trash and worthless. When you are working with materials like these, there may be a limited amount of fabric that you can use. Consider the quilt rug shown here. There was only one damaged quilt to be cut up and used for this rug. It's not like you have an unlimited source for your rag strips. If you were using new fabric from the fabric store and you ran out, you could simply go back and buy some more. When you are planning for a rug like this, however, you have to preplan how you are going to weave it. If you were planning to use only this quilt for the weft strips, well, when you had woven the last rag strip, you would be done weaving the rug. It can only be as long in length as you have rag strips to weave it. If you were hoping to weave a long hall runner, you'd better plan to add rags from another source, ones that will complement your quilt rags. If I am using new fabric for a rug, I calculate one yard of fabric to weave a square foot of rag carpeting. When you are working with recycled materials, you might do better to rely on weight of materials to estimate what you need. I would suggest that you plan on three to four pounds of rags to weave a rug approximately two feet by three feet. Keep good records of what you have used. This will prove to be beneficial for your future rugs.

You will notice that I have not included any warp lengths with the drafts. That was with purpose. You and I will likely have very different ideas on how long you want your finished rug to be. *You are going to have to do some homework on your own*, but let me help you out here: Calculate how long you want your finished rug to be. Add 20% for take-up. Then add 5–6 inches for the hem allowance (12 inches if you want fringe on your rug). This is how long your warp should be for one rug. If you want to weave several rugs on the same warp, multiply the sum for one rug by how many you want to weave. Now add 36 inches for loom waste. That's your total warp length.

Some last words of advice: Enjoy yourself! Once you start to look around and see all the possibilities of materials you can use for rag rugs, you are going to go crazy weaving rugs.

The original damaged quilt

As with this quilt rug, sometimes your rug size will be determined by the amount of material you have.

Projects

1 | Better Days

A friend asked me whether there was any way of reweaving an old favorite rug that she had used in her kitchen for many years. It was originally woven with cotton carpet warp and wool strips from numerous old blankets. The rug had been machine washed many times and the cotton threads had just given out. The warp threads were torn and broken, and the rag weft was now exposed.

The answer is YES! The weft was perfectly felted and still usable. We pulled the cotton threads out of the old rug and wound the old weft strips onto rug shuttles. We chose a new warp color arrangement and warped her loom. She then rewove the old felted wool strips back into a new rug. Now how's that for recycling?

This warp arrangement would be fine for any rags that you want to weave into it. Change the colors out to personalize it to your liking. Remember that there are no wrong choices that you can make. It would be smart to put on enough warp for several rugs. Change out the weft materials at your discretion.

The original
damaged rug

Threading

C				B				B				A				A			
	C				C				B				B				A		
		C				B				B				A				A	
			C				C				B				B				A
10x				2x				10x				2x				10x			

Threading (cont.)

A				B				B				C				C				D				D				C			
	A				A				B				B				C				C				D				D		
		A				B				B				C				C				D				D				C	
			A				A				B				B				C				C				D				D
10x				2x				10x				2x				10x				2x				10x				2x			

Tie-up

	4		
3			
	2		
1			
x		4x	Hem
	x		
	x	5x	
x			
x		6x	
	x		
x		Body of rug	
	x		
x		6x	Hem
	x		
	x	5x	
x			
x		4x	
	x		

WARP

8/4 cotton carpet warp

Colors:

Color A: Gold, 88 ends

Color B: Copper, 96 ends

Color C: Colonial Green, 96 ends

Color D: Olive Green, 48 ends

Total ends: 328

Sett

12 epi

Width in Reed

27.3 inches

WEFT

Hems

2 strands of 8/4 cotton wound together

Rug Body

Recycled wool rags originally cut to 1-inch-wide strips

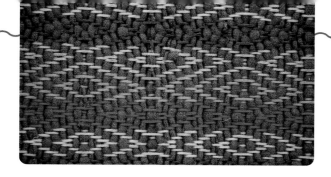

2 | Autumn Moss

When you decide to do some deep cleaning around the house, be aware that you might come upon some treasures that you completely forgot about. This was the case when I went through a blanket chest in the spare bedroom. The blanket chest had become something of a catchall and also a stand for the television in that room. It had been years since I lifted the lid and went through the contents of that chest. When I did, I came upon a dark green, woolen army blanket. Where it came from, I haven't a clue, because my father didn't serve in the army. I do remember, when I was a boy, using this scratchy blanket when sleeping in a pup tent in the backyard. My family didn't go on vacations, but when sleeping in that tent, I used my imagination to take me to national parks and wild places. The experience was exciting and all just a hundred feet from the back kitchen door.

When I looked at that old army blanket, I noticed it was worn and had some damage from wool moths. I thought, "What's the sense in keeping this old blanket?" Then it hit me: that old army blanket would make a wonderful rag rug. The thick texture of the blanket would make a strong and hard-wearing rug. Its dark olive drab color would make a great background color for a brightly colored warp.

I chose bright fall colors for the warp and threaded and treadled it to a Twill arrangement. To prepare the rag strips, I cut them with a rug cutter to about an inch wide. You could also use scissors or a rotary cutter to cut your strips. The thick and dense material didn't allow the tearing technique that I usually use to make fabric strips.

The resulting rug turned out well, don't you think? That old blanket brings back lots of happy memories. To think I nearly discarded it! I would be happy to put that rug back into my home now or even on the damp ground of a pup tent.

The old army blanket that became the weft

Threading

(F)			4		4			4			4			4			4		4			(F)
		3				3			3				3			3				3		
	2						2			2			2				2				2	
1				1			1		1			1			1			1				1

Balance last time ←————————— 10x —————————→

Tie-up

		4	4		4
	3	3		3	
2	2				2
1			1	1	
				x	
					x
x					
	x				
		x			
			x		
x					
			x		
		x			
	x				

Color Order

18				18	Loden
			18		Bronze Gold
		18			Cardinal
	18				Burnt Orange
18					Khaki

←——— 4x ———→

WARP

8/4 cotton carpet warp

Colors:

Loden, 90 ends plus 4 for floating selvedge (F)

Bronze Gold, 72 ends

Cardinal, 72 ends

Burnt Orange, 72 ends

Khaki, 72 ends

Total ends: 378 + 4 = 382

Sett

16 epi, 2 per dent in an 8-dent reed

Note: Sley 2 ends per dent and 2 ends in a heddle.

Width in Reed

23.875 inches

WEFT

Hems

2 strands of 8/4 cotton wound together; woven in Plain Weave

Rag Body

Wool blanket cut into 1-inch-wide strips

The colorful warp threads

3 | Rose Garden

I have fallen in love with the rag rug traditions of Sweden and other parts of Scandinavia. These rugs are often woven with a weft-face emphasis. This example is woven like Overshot with a pattern row alternating with Tabby rows. What makes this different from traditional Overshot is that the rug is woven entirely with rag wefts. Traditional Overshot is based on a Twill threading and is woven with two separate weft threads. A heavier-weight thread is typically woven as the pattern thread and following a Twill order. A Tabby thread that is usually the same size thread as the warp thread alternates between the pattern wefts. Here, in the style of fabulous Scandinavian rugs, the pattern rags and the Tabby rags are both cut or torn into narrow rags of about ¾ inches wide.

I found three solid-colored flannel sheets in burgundy, medium blue, and cream. They were all queen-sized sheets, so I knew I would have enough rag material to weave a rug. I tore all the rags to a ¾-inch width. There are areas of Plain Weave alone and carefully placed areas of Overshot patterning.

Follow the pattern treadling as seen in the draft. I finished the rug with a Damascus edge and twisted fringe.

Rose Garden
on the loom

Threading

4		4					4		4		4		4		4							
					3		3		3								3		3		3	
				2		2		2												2		2		2
	1		1		1							1		1						1		1

← 7x →
← Balance last time →

Tie-up

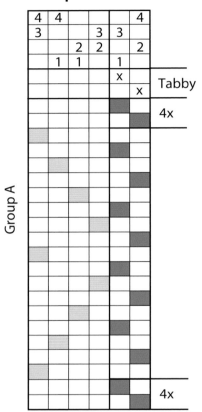

Group A

4	4				4
3			3	3	
		2	2		2
	1	1		1	
				x	
					x	Tabby

4x (top)
4x (bottom)

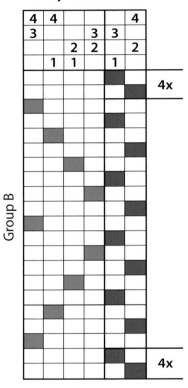

Group B

4	4				4
3			3	3	
		2	2		2
	1	1		1	

4x (top)
4x (bottom)

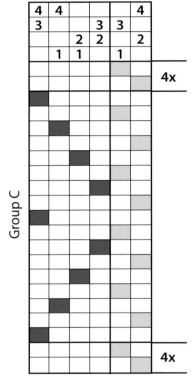

Group C

4	4				4
3			3	3	
		2	2		2
	1	1		1	

4x (top)
4x (bottom)

WARP
12/6 Seine Twine, Fiskgarn, Swedish cotton warp in Blue

Total ends: 205

Sett
8 epi

Width in Reed
25.6 inches

WEFT
Beginning and Ending of Rug
12/6 blue cotton doubled for 4 picks of Tabby

Body of Rug
Flannel sheets cut to ¾-inch-wide strips

Colors:
- ■ Blue
- ▨ Cream
- ■ Wine

Weave as Tabby and Twill pattern picks.

Weave the A-B-C groups as many times as desired. End with Group A to balance.

4 | Diamonds & Roses

This rug was woven on the same warp as Rose Garden (page 19). I used only two colors for my wefts. The Tabby, or Plain Weave, background is medium blue, and the pattern weft is a rich wine color.

Unlike traditional Overshot that uses a fine Tabby thread and a heavier-weight pattern thread, this style of rag weaving uses rag wefts of the same width. You will love these sturdy rugs.

I finished this rug with a simple overhand knotted fringe.

On the loom

Threading

4		4						4		4		4		4		4							
					3		3		3						3		3		3				
			2		2		2											2		2		2		
	1		1		1						1		1									1		1

← 7x →

← Balance last time →

WARP

12/6 Seine Twine, Fiskgarn, Swedish cotton warp in Blue

Total ends: 205

Sett

8 epi

Width in Reed

25.6 inches

WEFT

Flannel sheets cut to ¾-inch-wide strips

Colors:

- ▢ Blue—Tabby Weft
- ▢ Wine—Pattern Weft

Tie-up

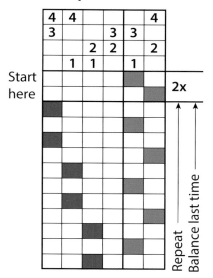

Start here

2x

Repeat / Balance last time

Tie-up

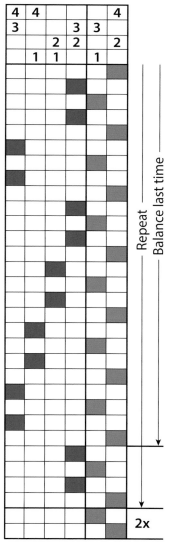

Repeat / Balance last time

2x

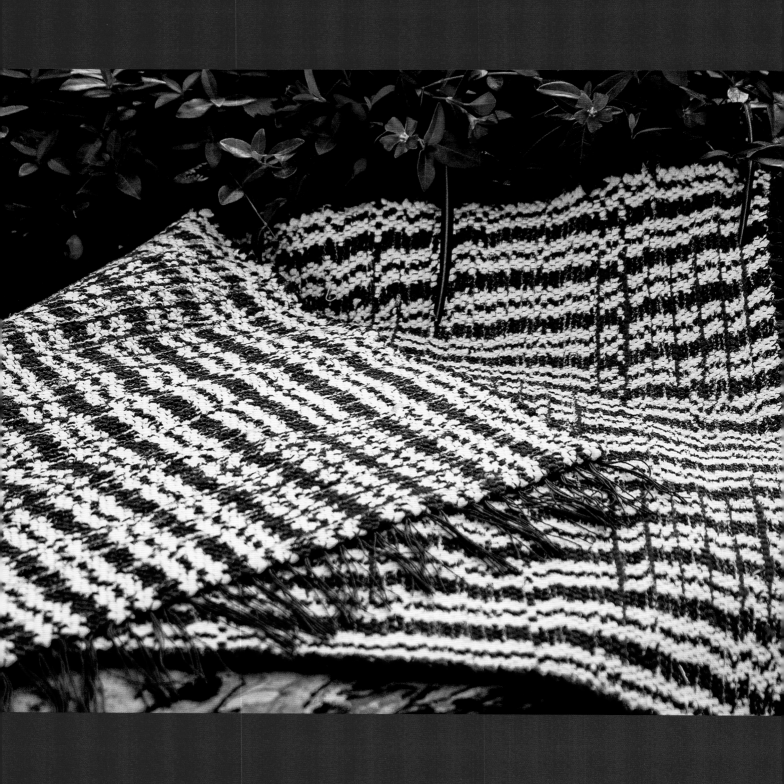

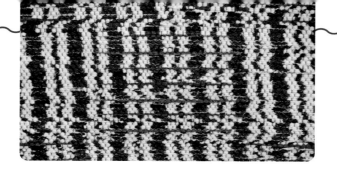

5 | Zuko

I had just finished weaving a rug with strips of wine-colored flannel fabric. I had thrown the tapered end pieces from the strips into the trash, thinking I wouldn't have any more use for those little snippets of fabric. Little did I know that they would become the focus of my next rug.

I had been given a set of sheets that had navy blue and white stripes running in the direction of headboard to footboard. I thought, "If I cut the fabric strips in the direction of the stripes, I will end up with a pile of navy-blue strips and white strips. If I cut them across the stripes, I will have strips with navy and white dashes that could be much more interesting." Then I thought, "If I carefully line up the blue segments as closely as possible, I can restore the original pattern." I tried it, and it worked. I wove a few inches and adjusted the fabric strips with each pick of weft. I carefully stacked up the blue areas in the open shed, and when I was pleased with the alignment, I closed the shed to trap the strip in place and then beat it down.

I then looked down into the trash can and saw all those little snippets of wine-colored, tapered flannel waste pieces. I retrieved them from the trash and decided to place them into the open shed from time to time to create a pattern. I opened a shed, threw the striped strip, and beat it into place. With the same shed open, I then worked and placed a wine-colored snippet into the web with my hands and placed it where I wanted it to appear.

I wove a checkerboard pattern, but you could weave these little snippets into your work in a random pattern, too. Anything goes.

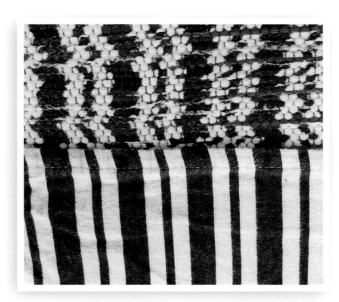

The stripes on the rug correspond to the stripes in the sheets used for weft

Threading

4			4			4		
	3			3			3	
		2			2			2
			1			1			1

Tie-up

	4
3	
	2
1	
x	
	x
x	
	x

WARP

  12/6 Seine Twine, Fiskgarn, Swedish cotton warp in Blue

Total ends: 200

Sett

  8 epi

Width in Reed

  25 inches

WEFT

  Striped flannel sheets cut to ¾-inch-wide strips, plus narrow 4- to 5-inch-long scraps of rags to lay into the open shed randomly

Zuko, the cat, approves of the stripes

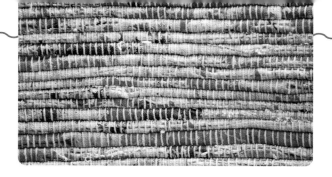

6 | Dry Paint

When my wife and I bought our new home, we agreed that the house needed to be painted in a more neutral color palette. We agreed that before we moved a single thing into the house, we would hire a painter. One day I decided to pop in at lunchtime to see how the painting was coming along. When I walked into the house and looked around, I was taken aback by all the paint-splotched drop cloths that were strewn over our hardwood floors.

Wow, it looked like I had walked right into Jackson Pollock's studio. I remember reading how Pollock painted in a very small shed when he started working on his large-scale paintings. He would lay a canvas on the floor of the shed and then walk around the perimeter of the canvas, dripping and throwing paint onto the surface, adding layers and layers of different colors of paint to achieve the look that pleased him. The drop cloths protecting our floors looked just like one of those early paintings.

I was so excited about the yards of fabric with all those paint drips, I forgot to look at the walls of our home and give thanks to the painter who did such a fabulous job. I couldn't get past the possibility of cutting those drop cloths into strips for rugs.

When our house painting was finished, I was fortunate enough to talk the painter into giving up one of those beautiful drop cloths. I explained my intention for the drop cloth, which luckily for me he found absolutely fascinating, and he gave me one of his oldest and most dripped-on tarps.

After examining the drop cloth, my friend Kathy (who is also this book's photographer and a weaving helper) decided that the fabric needed a little more color and took it upon herself to go "Pollock" on it and add some more splatters of brightly colored paint to it. The result was nothing less than wonderful, and the cutting of the strips was so much fun.

I randomly wove the strips of painted canvas into the neutral-colored cotton warp. I wove the rug in a simple Plain Weave so as not to distract from the beautiful colors of the fabric strips.

I think this rug is a winner in two categories: one for durability and the second for a most unique use of an unlikely source of materials.

Threading

L				E				T			
	E					T				L	
		T					L				E
			L					E				T

◄——————— 25x ———————►

Tie-up

	4
3	
	2
1	

x		4x
	x
	x	5x
x	
x		6x
	x

Hem

x	
	x
x		Body of Rug
	x

x	
	x	6x
	x	5x
x	
x		4x
	x

Hem

WARP
8/4 cotton carpet warp

Colors:
Linen, 100 ends
Ecru, 100 ends
Tan, 100 ends
Total ends: 300

Sett
12 epi

Width in Reed
25 inches

WEFT

Hems
2 strands of 8/4 cotton wound together

Body of Rug
Cotton canvas cut to 1-inch-wide strips

Neutral warp threads in Linen, Ecru, and Tan

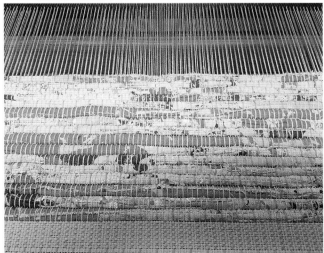
On the loom

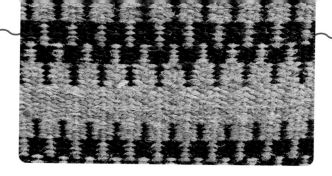

7 | Krokbragd

Krokbragd is a Scandinavian technique of weaving weft-face Twill. What makes it unique is that it is a three-shaft Twill weave, not the typical four-shaft Boundweave Twill. It is woven with a very open sett so that the weft can beat down and cover the warp thread completely.

I found three cotton sheets that I thought would be perfect for this rug, one each in navy blue, light blue, and pink. They all complemented each other nicely. I tore the sheets into ¾-inch-wide strips. I then wove the strips following the draft shown here. I finished the warp ends with a Damascus edge and then twisted the fringe.

Threading

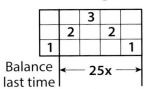

Balance last time ← 25x →

Tie-up

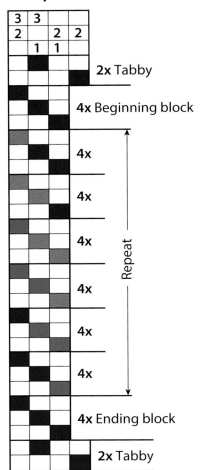

2x Tabby

4x Beginning block

4x

4x

4x

4x

4x

4x

Repeat

4x Ending block

2x Tabby

WARP

12/6 Natural Cotton

Total ends: 202

Sett

8 epi (4 working epi)

Note: Sley 2 ends per dent and 2 in each heddle.

WEFT

Cotton sheets cut in ¾-inch-wide strips

Colors:

☐ Navy

☐ Medium Blue

☐ Pink

8 | Checkmate

Years ago, I was introduced to thick yarn from Sweden known as string garn. It was made by stranding numerous thinner threads together to make a heavier-weight yarn. Sometimes you hear it referred to as mop cotton. I thought, at the time, that it was quite expensive to buy and that I could probably make my own yarn by simply stranding several threads of my liking together.

I started by choosing threads of all the same type: all cotton, all linen, or all wool. Later I discovered that it didn't matter what I combined because they supported each other. There wasn't a problem with differential shrinkage. The colors I put together played a bigger role in how it looked, I discovered.

For this rug, I started out by making two piles of threads: dark colors and light colors. The yarns that I stranded were 8/4, 8/2, 3/2, 5/2—any odd-sized yarns. These just all happened to be 100% cotton threads. I kept adding to the groups until the stranded threads were about the size of a pencil.

When I felt I had just the correct amount, I put the cones into a box to keep them from rolling around on the floor. I took the multiple threads and wound them together onto a rug shuttle.

To my amazement, it didn't take a lot of yardage from any single source to make a lot of string yarn. If a thread runs out, simply tie a new thread to the end of the one you just lost. It doesn't even have to be the same size or color.

Threading

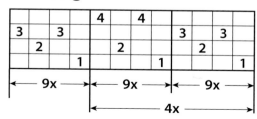

4			4		4				
3		3					3		3
	2				2			2	
			1			1			1

← 9x → ← 9x → ← 9x →

← 4x →

WARP

8/4 cotton carpet warp in Cardinal

Total ends: 324

Sett

12 epi

Width in Reed

27 inches

WEFT

Hems

2 strands of 8/4 cotton wound together

Body of Rug

Light and dark "string yarn," made by stranding multiple threads together until they are the thickness of a pencil

---

Tie-up

4	4				4	
		3	3		3	
	2		2	2		
1		1		1		
				x		4x
					x	4x
					x	5x
				x		5x
				x		6x
					x	6x
D						
			L			8x
	D					8x
		L				8x
L						
			D			8x
	L					8x
		D				8x
D						
			L			8x
	D					8x
		L				8x
				x		6x
					x	6x
					x	5x
				x		5x
				x		4x
					x	4x

Hem

Repeat

Hem

9 | Mountain Meadows

Weaving with loopers is nothing new to the weaving community. "What are loopers?" you may ask. They are the waste material that's cut from the tops of athletic socks. You might recall using them to make pot holders when you were a child. Brightly colored knitted sock loopers are stretched over teeth on a frame in a North/South direction. This becomes the warp. You then weave loopers in the East/West direction, securing the loopers on pegs that line the left and right sides of the frame. When you are finished weaving your pot holder, you remove the pot holder from the loom and secure the edges by interlocking the loops. These are still a very popular way of weaving for young and old alike.

I see these cotton sock loops as a great rug weft. A weft that will weave up into a thick and durable rug that has the softness of socks and feels like terrycloth under your feet. It is a great use for what is considered factory waste.

I used loopers dyed in multiple shades of reds and berry colors. I took some time to first interlock the loopers, putting about 20 loopers together to make a continuous length that would comfortably fit on my rug shuttle. (See the photos to better understand how to interlock them.) When I came to the end of the materials on my shuttle, I attached the next group of loopers to the last group by passing the shuttle through the last loop and then back on itself again to attach them.

They are fun to weave, and you can find sock loopers in many weaving supply stores that sell rug weaving materials and pot holder looms.

Threading

4			4		
	3			3	
		2			2
			1			1

Tie-up

	4
3	
	2
1	
x		**2x** Beginning header
	x	
x		Body of rug
	x	
x		
	x	
x		**2x** Ending header
	x	

WARP

12/6 Seine Twine, Fiskgarn, Swedish cotton warp in Natural

Total ends: 200

Sett

8 epi (4 working epi)

Note: Sley 2 ends in each dent and heddle.

Width in Reed

25 inches

WEFT

Beginning and Ending Headers

2 strands of 8/4 cotton wound together

Body of Rug

Dyed sock loopers, interlocked

Finished with Damascus edge (i.e., the ends worked back into the edge of the rug)

Interlocking loopers

Damascus edge

10 | Christmas Past

When people know you appreciate old textiles, they often look to you as the keeper of their treasured heirloom. Such is the story behind this old quilt. The owner knew that it took a long time to make and should have a place of honor in their home, but they didn't want it (or even like it), and their kids didn't want it either. Where do you go with such a treasure? It's a dilemma.

When the quilt's owner gave it to me, they apologized for the tears and worn spots in the quilt. They said, "It's in bad shape, but we thought you might like to have it. Do what you want with it."

It was in bad condition, with holes and rips, and not anything you would want to put on your guest bed. I saw it as a source of fabric. "This could make a lot of fabric strips," I thought.

I designed and wound a warp in colors that complemented the colors in the quilt. My dear friend Kathy said she would love to weave the rug. Kathy washed the quilt and then started cutting the fabric strips, working around the tears and holes. As she did, the cotton quilt batting dropped out, leaving her with just the stitched top and backing of the quilt as her strips. Kathy randomly chose the quilt strips as she wove the rug. I think it's a very pretty rag rug and perfect for a child's bedroom. This old worn-out quilt has now been repurposed and is again something beautiful to look at.

Color Order

Duck 108																	
12		12		12		12		12		12		12		12		12	Duck 108
	12		12				12		12				12		12		Old Rose 72
					60					60							Red 120

Threading

4				4				4			
	3				3				3		
		2				2				2	
			1				1				1

Tie-up

	4
3	
	2
1	
x	
	x
x	
	x
x	
	x

WARP
8/4 cotton carpet warp
Colors:
Duck, 108 ends
Old Rose, 72 ends
Red, 120 ends
Total ends: 300
Sett
12 epi
Width in Reed
25 inches
WEFT
Hems
2 strands of 8/4 cotton wound together
Body of Rug
Old quilt cut into 1-inch-wide strips

Warp colors were chosen to coordinate with the quilt

Quilt in its used condition

11 | Thrums Up

Thrums are the leftover lengths of thread passing through the reed and heddles and attached to the apron rod in the back of the loom when you have come to the last of your warp. Barry Schacht once told me, "Crumbs are the leftover bits of bread. Thrums are the crumbs of thread." That makes perfect sense to me and always makes me smile when I think of it.

This rug was woven with the thrums of other rag rug warps. The weft consists of 12 strands of 8/4 carpet warp tied into bundles, end to end, to make a long length. After tying several bundles together, I wound them onto a rug shuttle. After a length of thrum weft was woven, I simply tied on a new shuttle of thrums.

I saved warp thrums from several projects. These original warps were sett at 12 epi. I made sure that I tied them in 1-inch groups (12 threads) of warp onto the rear apron rod. This made an equal thickness of thrums to tie together later, which became the weft for this rug. Having a warp of multiple colors makes for interesting thrum bundles. Don't worry about the knots. They will add interest to the overall look of your rugs. Enjoy!

On the loom

Threading

4				4				4			
	3				3				3		
		2				2				2	
			1				1				1

Tie-up

	4	
3		
	2	
1		
x		Header
	x	
x		
	x	Body of rug
x		
	x	
x		
	x	Header

WARP

12/6 Seine Twine, Fiskgarn, Swedish cotton warp in Blue

Total ends: 200 + 8 selvedge = 208

Sett

8 epi

Note: Double first and last 4 ends in dents and heddles for selvedge treatment.

Width in Reed

25 inches

WEFT

Headers

2 strands of 8/4 cotton wound together

Body of Rug

Thrums of 8/4 cotton tied together

Thrums are the leftover lengths of thread when you have come to the last of your warp, otherwise known as loom waste.

12 | Denim Days

Ilove denim for its strength and durability. I have been wearing blue jeans for as long as I can remember. The older they are, the more worn and comfortable they become. At a certain point, though, you need to say goodbye to your old friend. I get a lot of satisfaction in knowing that I can recycle these jeans into rag rugs.

For years I cut the legs off and cut 1-inch fabric strips lengthwise. I didn't like (or I thought I didn't like) the seams running in the strips. I have changed my mind on that sort of thinking. For this rag rug, I cut spiral fabric strips from the legs. Not only does this approach give long lengths of fabric, but the bumpy seams also give nice textural interest to the finished rug. I have come to like those textured bumps a lot.

Weaving strips cut from several pairs of jeans with different degrees of wear makes for a great-looking rug. You could weave this as Plain Weave, and it would be lovely. I decided to try a thick-and-thin Rep Weave in a colorway that would complement the jean strips. Try using different-colored denim jeans. The possibilities are endless.

Threading

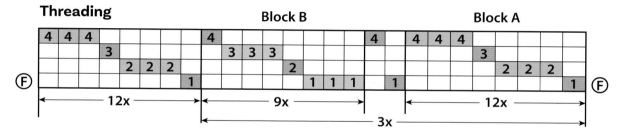

Block B   Block A

4	4	4							4									4		4	4	4			
			3								3	3	3										3		
				2	2	2									2									2	2
							1							1	1	1		1							1

F ← |—— 12x ——| |—— 9x ——| |—— 12x ——| → F

|——————————————— 3x ———————————————|

Tie-up

	4
3	
	2
1	

x		
	x	4x
	x	5x
x		
x		6x
	x	
F		
	H	16x
F		
	F	12x
H		
	F	
F		
	H	16x
x		
	x	6x
	x	5x
x		
x		4x
	x	

Hem (top 4x, 5x, 6x)

5x

Balance last time

Hem (bottom 6x, 5x, 4x)

WARP

8/4 cotton carpet warp

Colors:

- Velvet, 288 ends
- Loden Green, 162 ends
- Spanish Blue, 156 ends + 2 ends for floating selvedges = 158

Total ends: 608

Sett

24 epi, 2 per dent in a 12-dent reed

Width in Reed

25.25 inches

WEFT

Hems

2 strands of Velvet wound together

Body of Rug

H = blue jeans cut to ¾-inch-wide strips

F = 8/4 cotton in Spanish Blue

Cutting jean legs in a spiral

13 | Smooth Sailing

My wife and I love to cruise. Cindy has traveled to many parts of the world with Holland American Line. It didn't take much to convince me that this was a spectacular way to see the world. As your ship pulls away, you leave the stresses of life behind you back in port. You immediately relax. I have found some of my best ideas come during a poolside lunch with an umbrella drink.

On a recent cruise, our ship anchored off a lovely island where we took a tender to a beautiful sandy beach for some sun, swimming, and a delicious catered lunch. After a dip in the turquoise-colored water, I went to dry off with one of the towels from the ship. I looked at the towel, and there, across the ends, were the words *Holland America Line*. Wide white and blue stripes made up the body of the Turkish towel. When I held the towel in my hand, I knew that it would make a great rug if it was cut into strips. But how could I possibly get hold of several of these towels? Enough to weave a rug? "Surely, they must have some that are getting a little worn from wear," I thought.

When we returned to the ship, I asked our cabin steward whether there might be someone whom I could talk to about acquiring several of the towels. He directed me to talk to the guest service associate. I met with a lovely associate named Rose and explained that I was writing a book about weaving rag rugs. The theme for the book was to use only unwanted or used materials and to recycle them into rag rugs. I explained my idea to use torn or damaged Holland America towels for one of the many rug projects that would appear in my book. I asked if it was possible to obtain several of the used cruise line towels. Rose asked for our cabin number and said she would see what she could do for me.

The next day, there was a small stack of clean and folded towels with holes and tears in them on our bed. A note was attached that read, "Compliments of Holland America. We hope this will work for your rug, Mr. Knisely. Sincerely, Rose."

You can only imagine how thrilled I was to get hold of the towels. Before we got our feet back onto home soil, I had already designed a warp to go with the towel's colors. The warp would be made up of colors that I remembered of the beautiful Caribbean Sea. I saw that woven monogram on the edge of the towel that read "Holland America Line" and thought, "This will make a great hem at the end of the rug." I measured the monogram and added 10% to that measurement to determine the warp's width in the reed. There is always some degree of draw-in as you weave, and this worked out perfectly.

I wove a hem on either side of the rug. After rolling the hem, Cindy stitched the towel monogram onto the rug. It has made a fun reminder of a wonderful vacation that we spent in the Caribbean.

Turkish towels make a nice, thick rag rug. Be sure to cut the rugs weft strips outdoors. There is a lot of lint that comes from the cutting of these tufted pile woven towels. There will be enough lint created that you don't want the mess inside your home.

I hope you enjoy recycling your old bath or beach towels and giving them new life as an absorbent bathroom rug.

Threading

J			P			B				J				B			P		
	P			B				J			J				B			P	
		B			J				P			P			J				B
			J			P				B			P			J			B

|← 3x →|← 3x →|
|← 5x →|

Threading (cont.)

J			B			P		
	J			B			P	
		P			J			B
			P		J			B

|← 3x →|
Balance

Tie-up

	4
3	
	2
1	

x			
	x	4x	
	x	5x	Hem
x			
x			
	x	6x	
x			
	x		
x			Body of rug
	x		
x			
	x	6x	
	x	5x	Hem
x			
x			
	x	4x	

WARP

8/4 cotton carpet warp

Colors:

Royal Blue (**B**), 132 ends

Peacock (**P**), 132 ends

Jade (**J**), 132 ends

Total ends: 396

Sett

12 epi

Width in Reed

33 inches

WEFT

Hems

2 strands of 8/4 cotton wound together

Body of Rug

Towels cut to 1-inch-wide strips

My precious stack of Holland America beach towels

Warp in the colors of the Caribbean Sea

Stitched hem reminder of happy days at sea

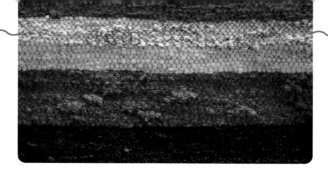

14 | Woolly Bear

The fiber arts community went crazy when they saw Bernie Sanders's knit mittens at the 2021 inauguration. The mittens were made from repurposed sweaters. Wool sweaters were first felted by agitating them in the washing machine in hot, soapy water. They were then dried in the clothes dryer, which makes for an otherwise perfect disaster. The sweater shrinks and tightens up, but the knitted pattern is still very visible. This felted wool fabric is now ready to be cut and made into awesome mittens.

A felted sweater is normally a disappointing moment, but if you can cut it into strips and use it as a rug weft, well, this item might have some merit and make me feel better about sweaters that have lost their original shape and size. I thought I would give it a try. I put a shout out to friends and family that I was looking for 100% wool sweaters to felt. They could be any size or color. They could have snags or tears, and I would even take them with some moth holes. After the abuse I was about to give them, no wool moth would have a chance of survival.

I was fortunate to receive quite a few very worthy donations.

After felting the sweaters, I cut them with scissors into 1-inch-wide strips. I found pullover sweaters with long sleeves to be the best candidates. I carefully spiral cut these sweaters to get long continuous strips.

I wound the cut strips into balls, and when the time came to weave the felted knit strips, I randomly mixed the colors as I wove them. My only rule was not to weave two like-colored strips one after another and to use contrasting colors alternatingly.

I want to give you a word of warning: There is a lot of lint involved with the cutting and weaving of these strips. You will make a mess, and you might want to wear a mask as you weave so as to not inhale a lot of dust. Otherwise, enjoy the fun.

Threading

4				4				4			
	3				3				3		
		2				2				2	
			1				1				1

Tie-up

	4	
3		
	2	
1		
x		**4x** Header
	x	
x		
	x	Body of rug
x		
	x	
x		
	x	**4x** Header

WARP

12/6 Seine Twine, Fiskgarn, Swedish cotton warp in Blue

Total ends: 200

Sett

8 epi

Note: Double sley the first and last four dents; thread the doubled ends as one in the heddles.

Width in Reed

24 inches

WEFT

Beginning and Ending Headers

8 picks with 12/6 Seine Twine

Body of Rug

Felted sweaters cut to 1-inch-wide strips

Felted sweater strips wound into balls, ready for weaving

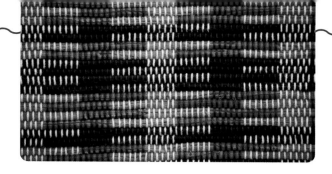

15 | Summer Showers

Every now and then you need a change around the house—so it was with two bathrooms that needed a fresh look. One had a navy blue shower curtain and the other a burgundy one. The two curtains complemented each other, and together they would make a lot of rag strips. I thought if I wove the colors in a random order, I could make a nice rug.

I warped the loom to the draft seen here. When I am warping, I always consider the time it takes to warp a loom. Why not warp for two rugs? That is what I did, and you will see that the draft for the Rhapsody in Blue rug (page 57) is the same as this draft. I used a plaid cotton for the weft in Rhapsody in Blue. They look totally different, don't they? I love a good two-for-one warp opportunity.

The same warp was used for Summer Showers and Rhapsody in Blue

Threading

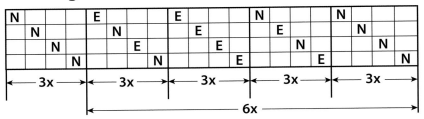

Tie-up

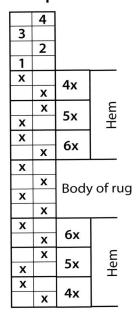

WARP

8/4 cotton carpet warp

Colors:

Navy (**N**), 156 ends

Ecru (**E**), 144 ends

Total ends: 300

Sett

12 epi

Width in Reed

25 inches

WEFT

Hems

2 strands of 8/4 cotton in Navy wound together

Body of Rug

Old shower curtains cut into 1-inch-wide strips

16 | Rhapsody in Blue

My neighbors remembered I was working on a book on recycling materials for rag rugs, and they offered me this lovely piece of plaid fabric that had been chewed by mice. It was to be a coat, but the mice had chewed a large hole right in the middle of the bolt. It wasn't much good for a coat now, but it was perfect for a rug.

The arrangement of the plaid pattern made it easy to see where to cut the rags. I cut deep, 1-inch-wide slits into the fabric to start. I then tore the strips lengthwise to get nice long fabric strips to weave.

This rug was woven on the same warp as Summer Showers (page 55). This warp would work for many fabric strips that you would want to weave into it. Change out the colors to suit your taste.

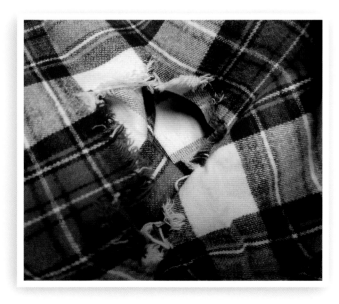

Threading

N			E		E		N		N		
	N			N		E		E		N	
		N			E		E		N		N
			N			N		E		E		N

← 3x → ← 3x → ← 3x → ← 3x → ← 3x →

← 6x →

Tie-up

	4	
3		
	2	
1		
x		
	x	4x
	x	
x		5x
x		
	x	6x
x		Body of rug
	x	
x		
	x	
x		
	x	6x
	x	
x		5x
x		
	x	4x

Hem (top 4x, 5x, 6x)
Body of rug
Hem (bottom 6x, 5x, 4x)

WARP

8/4 cotton carpet warp

Colors:

Navy (**N**), 156 ends

Ecru (**E**), 144 ends

Total ends: 300

Sett

12 epi

Width in Reed

25 inches

WEFT

Hems

2 strands of 8/4 cotton in Navy wound together

Body of Rug

Flannel fabric cut to 1-inch-wide strips

17 | Where's the Warp?

This rug is an example of weft-face weaving. The warp has an open sett so that the weft rags pack down and completely cover the warp. There is nothing complex about the weaving of this style of rug. It is woven in Plain Weave, and the bold stripes come from the different colored and patterned fabric rags that were used. I carefully chose fabrics with both cool colors and warm colors. I also wanted dark and light colors to give contrasting interest to the stripes. When I was ready to design the stripe pattern, I made the stripes of different widths and was careful to put cool colors against the warmer colors. Darker colors framed the lighter colors. This arrangement is very pleasing to the eye and adds a lot of interest.

There is a planned repeating pattern to this rug. Take a look at the treadling to see the order of the rags.

Of course, you are not going to find the same fabric remnants that I used and show here. Look for colors that work best in your home. Follow the draft for ideas about stripe widths. You might have to make changes based on the amount of rags you have. Remember, there are no wrong choices here.

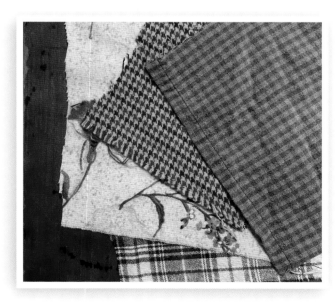

The fabric choices were varied in colors and textures

Threading

4			4			4		
	3			3			3	
		2			2			2
			1			1			1

Tie-up

	4
3	
	2
1	
x	
	x
x	
	x

# of picks	Color
24	Blue
6	Plaid
2	Camel
8	Floral
2	Camel
6	Plaid
24	Blue
24	Camel
6	Floral
2	Blue
6	Plaid
2	Blue
6	Floral
24	Camel

3x

Balance last time

WARP

12/6 Seine Twine, Fiskgarn, Swedish cotton warp in Natural

Total ends: 200

Sett

8 epi

Note: Double sley the first four and last four dents in the 8-dent reed; thread doubled ends as one in heddles.

Width in Reed

24 inches

WEFT

Headers

4 picks of 12/6 cotton

Body of Rug

4 different flannel fabrics cut to ¾-inch-wide strips

Fabric cut and wound into balls for weaving

18 | Pool's Open

Are you familiar with Shadow Weave? Perhaps you have woven this form of color and weave as a dish towel. Traditional Shadow Weave uses two contrasting colors in the warp and weft. The threading and the treadling are based on Twill. Most applications of Shadow Weave use the same size threads for both the warp and the weft, producing a fabric that is balanced. This means that there are the same number of weft picks per inch as there are warp ends per inch.

This rug uses a heavy-weight thread alternating with a finer thread in the same warp. To make a heavier thread, I simply put several strands of 8/4 cotton together and treated them as one thread. The finer thread in the draft is a single thread of 8/4 cotton. This creates the contrast in the warp direction rather than just a color contrast. The weft also uses a differential of sizes of weft materials to show the pattern. A heavy rag weft of old sheets alternates with a finer weft of doubled 8/4 cotton. This produces the contrast needed in the weft direction.

You will see areas that are warp emphasized and others that are weft emphasized. The weft-emphasized areas highlight and show the colors of the rags that you have woven in. The warp-emphasized blocks weave as weft-emphasized blocks on the back of the rug and vice versa. This makes it a true two-sided rug.

I looked for fabric colors that would complement the warp colors. For the rags, I found old sheets in the linen closet that had been forgotten for years. These were the sheets that my children used on their single beds or bunk beds. My children are grown and moved out of the house (along with their beds). It was time to put these unwanted sheets to a better use.

Use this draft as a guide and choose colors that best work for your home.

Profile Draft

		D					D	D				D	D						D			
	C					C	C				C	C								C		
B					B	B				B	B						B				B	
A			A	A				A	A	A					A	A						A

Tie-up

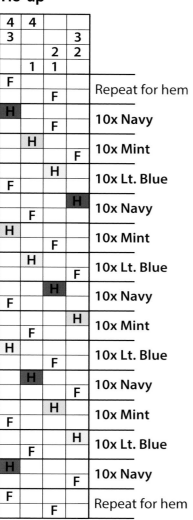

4	4		
3			3
		2	2
	1	1	

F				Repeat for hem
		F		
H				10x Navy
		F		
	H			10x Mint
			F	10x Lt. Blue
	H			
F				
			H	10x Navy
	F			
H				10x Mint
		F		
	H			10x Lt. Blue
			F	
F				10x Navy
		H		
	F			10x Mint
H				
		F		10x Lt. Blue
	H			10x Navy
			F	
	H			10x Mint
F				
		H		10x Lt. Blue
	F			
H				10x Navy
		F		
F				Repeat for hem
		F		

Key to Threading

Each square in the profile draft is equal to one pattern block.

Block D	4 4 4 / 2	6x
Block C	3 3 3 / 1	6x
Block B	4 / 2 2 2	6x
Block A	3 / 1 1 1	6x

WARP

8/4 cotton carpet warp

Colors:

- Aqua, 198 ends
- Spanish Blue, 144 ends
- Eggplant, 162 ends
- Orchid, 144 ends

Total ends: 648

Sett

24 epi (4 ends in a 6-dent reed)

Width in Reed

27 inches

WEFT

H = Cotton rags cut into 1½-inch-wide strips, in colors:

- Mint
- Light Blue
- Navy Blue

F = 2 strands of 8/4 cotton (one of each color) in colors:

- Aqua
- Eggplant

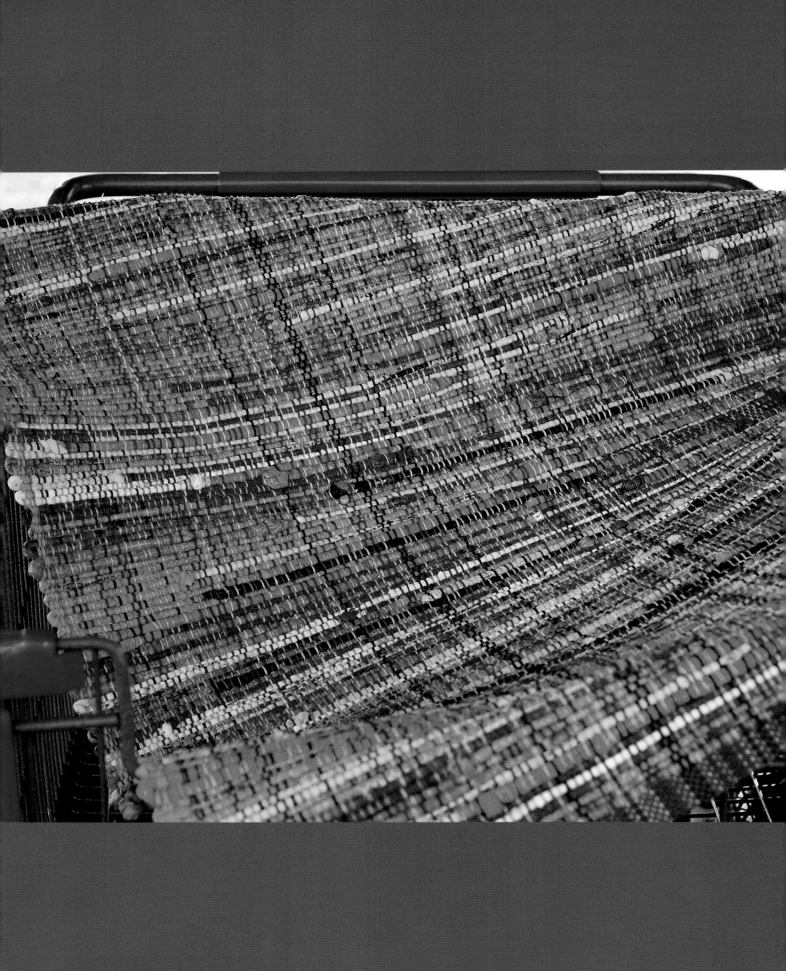

19 | Full Cart

My wife and I try to be good stewards of the Earth by using reusable shopping bags. Occasionally we slip and come home with the plastic bags provided at the store.

When I first heard about cutting and using plastic bags for yarn, people were using it to crochet mats and rugs for the homeless to get them off the cold ground and concrete streets. A student of mine told me that she was using different-colored plastic shopping bags as weft for rag rugs. She told me that these rugs work well by the back door, where her family comes in and out and are constantly bringing in mud and dirt on their shoes. She observed that different stores gave out different-colored bags. She said she liked mixing up the colored bags—light-colored bags and dark-colored bags and especially bags with bold graphic prints on them. To clean the rug when it gets dirty, simply shake out the dirt and hose it off outside. Then let it dry in the sun.

I thought, "What a great idea to show in a book about recycling used material for a good cause." I started by cutting bags across the middle, making plastic loops approximately 2 inches wide. I then interlocked the loops as you might do with sock loopers to make a continuous long length. If the bags seemed to be too thin, I used two together to strengthen it and make it thicker.

The warp was wound from many leftover spools of 8/4 carpet warp. The color arrangement was totally random, though I never put more than three ends of a color together, side by side. A total coat of many colors.

Display of the average American's plastic waste

Threading

4				4				4			
	3				3				3		
		2				2				2	
			1				1				1

Tie-up

	4		
3			
	2		
1			
x			
	x	4x	Hem
	x	5x	
x			
x		6x	
	x		
x			
	x		
x		Body of rug	
	x		
x			
	x	6x	Hem
	x	5x	
x			
x		4x	
	x		

WARP

8/4 cotton carpet warp in a random mix of many colors

Total ends: 300

Sett

12 epi

Width in Reed

25 inches

WEFT

Hems

2 strands of 8/4 cotton in blue wound together

Body of Rug

Plastic shopping bags in many colors

Two rugs, one warp: Full Cart (top) and Have You Any Wool? (bottom)

20 | Have You Any Wool?

My local weaver's guild held its annual "BAGRO" (bring and get rid of) party. This is when you have an opportunity to give away yarns and stuff you don't want any longer. A member had a plastic storage bin filled with rolls of precut wool fabric strips that he had intended to weave into rag rugs. Since he had had these rags for more years than he could remember and hadn't woven a single rug from them, he had decided it was time to move them on. Well, I gratefully gathered them up and brought them home.

The fabric seemed to be wool suiting fabric from men's and women's clothing. The pieces had started out as short lengths, but someone had sewn them together to make a continuous length, many yards long. The rolls were about 3 inches wide and nicely wound into a disk. These were going to be too wide for what I wanted, so I cut them lengthwise in half to a now more useable 1½ inches wide.

Wool rugs can easily be machine washed and air dried, although expect to have at least a 10% shrinkage the first time you wash them. They seem to be indestructible.

Threading

4			4			4		
	3			3			3	
		2			2			2
			1			1			1

Tie-up

	4		
3			
	2		
1			
x			Hem
	x	4x	
	x	5x	
x			
x		6x	
	x		
x			Body of rug
	x		
x			
	x		
x		6x	Hem
	x		
	x	5x	
x			
x		4x	
	x		

WARP

8/4 cotton carpet warp in a random mix of many colors

Total ends: 300

Sett

12 epi

Width in Reed

25 inches

WEFT

Hems

2 strands of 8/4 cotton in blue wound together

Body of Rug

Wool fabric strips cut into 1½-inch-wide strips

21 | Coffee with Cream

In *A Handweaver's Pattern Book* by Marguerite Porter Davison, I came upon a draft called Ginny's Coat. Its threading reminded me of another draft that I am very familiar with called Chicken Track Twill. I thought I might try this pattern, with a couple of variations to the draft, and weave Ginny's Coat as a rag rug. I rarely use the color brown in my weaving, but many people love the warm tones of brown and tan, so I thought I would try this colorway and weave it with just one rag color choice to highlight the pattern. You can see from the draft that it is composed of two parts. There is a section that weaves as a Broken Twill and another section that uses a three-end Point Twill. It is this three-end Point Twill that creates the chicken tracks. I decided to warp these two distinct areas in different colors to add a little interest to the rug.

Why not try a different color combination for your rug or even a solid-colored warp? It would make a pleasing-looking rug. It's a simple treadling to follow. Maybe you would like to warp for several rugs and use different colored rags—or try changing up the treadling given here for a different Twill variation.

I was given some old sheets that were a nice shade of chocolate brown. There were a few wears and tears to the sheets, best now to be recycled into rag strips. The warp coloration is very neutral and can accept a lot of different rag possibilities. You could put on a long warp and weave several rugs on the same warp. The rags could be very different, and yet they would all be related by a common warp arrangement. "Now, how cool is that?" I ask you.

Threading

Black   **Tan**   **Black**

4				4				4				4		4				4				4				4				4				4
	3					3				3			3					3					3				3				3			
		2					2		2			2		2					2		2			2				2		2				
			1					1				1					1					1				1				1				

(F) ... (F)

| Balance | ← 7x → | ← 8x → | Balance | ← 10x → | Balance | ← 7x → | ← 8x → |

← 3x →

Tie-up

		4	4		4		
	3	3		3			
2	2				2		
1			1	1			
			x				
				x		4x	
			x				
				x		5x	Hem
			x				
				x		6x	
x							
	x						
		x					Body of rug
			x				
			x				
				x		6x	
			x				
				x		5x	Hem
			x				
				x		4x	

WARP

8/4 cotton carpet warp

Colors:

Black, 252 ends + 2 for floating
    selvedges = 254

Tan, 189 ends

Total ends: 443

Sett

16 epi

Width in Reed

27.5 inches

WEFT

Hems

2 strands 8/4 cotton in tan wound
    together

Body of Rug

Medium-brown cotton fabric cut
    to 1½-inch-wide strips

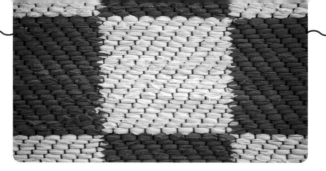

22 | Building Blocks

This threading draft is known by several names, including Block Twill, Turned Twill, and (in many older weavers' draft books) Twill Diaper Weave. An eighteenth-century weaver from Pennsylvania, Jacob Angstadt, had a manuscript devoted solely to Twill Diaper patterns.

I fell in love with this structure years ago and have used it many times for scarves, shawls, table linens, and baby blankets. Block Twill has a lot of versatility to its use, but the structure is shaft greedy, requiring four shafts to weave one pattern block and four shafts for each additional pattern block. Following and weaving a simple two-block profile draft will require eight shafts on your loom.

Here is how the structure works: One pattern block weaves as a 1/3 Twill while the other pattern block weaves as a 3/1 Twill. The first block is weft emphasized, and the other pattern block is warp emphasized. The tie-up can change that for you, though, and you can change the blocks to weave the other way. The other unique thing about this weave is the blocks appear to have their Twill lines moving in opposite directions. Hence the name, Turned Twill.

I have been interested in weaving two-sided rugs for quite a long time now. This requires just four shafts threaded to a simple straight draw Twill, which allows you to have two different rag wefts to appear on opposite sides of the rug. The rug is totally reversible and very cool. This treadling is called Stitched Double Cloth.

One day it occurred to me that I might be able to get two colors of rags to weave, side by side, in opposite blocks because of the Block Twill structure. When I looked at the tie-up, I found all the combinations needed to weave this. This rug is the result of my curious mind and some time to play with the structure. I hope you will try it.

Threading

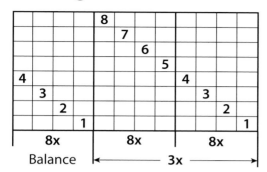

Tie-up

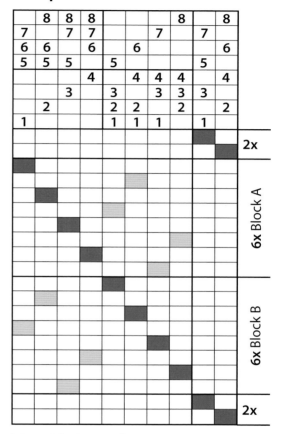

Weave Blocks **A** and **B** 6 times.
Weave Block **A** last time to balance.

WARP

12/6 Seine Twine, Fiskgarn, Swedish cotton warp in Dark Green

Total ends: 228 (224 working ends)

Sett

8 epi

Note: Sley double in the first two and last two ends in dent and heddles.

Width in Reed

28 inches

WEFT

Cotton rags cut into ¾-inch-wide strips, in two colors:

■ Red
▨ Beige

Log Cabin

Highland Cabin

23 | Log Cabin *and*
24 | Highland Cabin

While walking through an antique mall, I came across a roll of warp-face carpeting. It was about a yard wide and many yards long. The dealer who owned the rug told me that it came from a farm sale in Lancaster County, Pennsylvania, and had been used for years in the family's parlor.

I was intrigued by the simple warp-face color arrangement. It used two colors of blue alternating in a Log Cabin pattern. The two pattern blocks were separated with two light-colored threads. I didn't purchase the rug but asked whether I could take a picture of it to use as inspiration for a rug that I might want to weave sometime. Well, sometime is now, and I wanted to share it with you.

I used 8/4 cotton carpet warp for the warp. Take a look at the draft to see the color sequence in the threading and notice the two light-colored threads that separate the pattern blocks.

Warp-face rugs are very closely sett, which accounts for the many threads needed in the warp. I figured if I were going to thread hundreds of threads, I might as well weave two rugs on the same warp. The second rug is Highland Cabin.

What makes these two rugs so different is the weft materials. To stay true to the antique Amish rug, I wove the first rug with dark navy blue rags, much the same as the antique rug I first saw. The second rug used a bold plaid patterned fabric for the rag strips. The plaid fabric was in warm red and orange colors, which show through and contribute to the rug design.

The original antique rug that inspired the Log Cabin and Highland Cabin rugs

Threading

T		B				T		N			N			B			T	
		N			B				B			T			N			
			B					N				T			B			
	T			N	T				B			N			N	T		

← 6x → ← 6x →
← 10x →

Tie-up

		4
3		
		2
1		

x			
	x	4x	Hem
	x	5x	
x			
x		6x	
	x		
x			
	x		Body of rug
x			
	x		
x			
	x	6x	Hem
	x	5x	
x			
x			
	x	4x	

23 | LOG CABIN

WARP

8/4 cotton carpet warp

Colors:

Navy Blue (**N**), 272 ends

Moody Blue (**B**), 252 ends

Tan (**T**), 44 ends

Total ends: 568

Sett

24 epi

Width in Reed

23.5 inches

WEFT

Hems

2 strands of cotton in Navy wound together

Body of Rug

Cotton fabric in Navy Blue cut to 1½-inch-wide strips

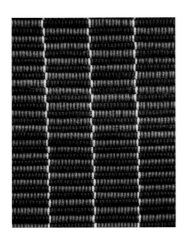

Threading

T		B				T		N			N			B			T	
		N			B				B			T			N			
			B					N				T			B			
	T			N	T				B			N			N	T		

← 6x → ← 6x →
← 10x →

Tie-up

		4
3		
		2
1		

x			
	x	4x	Hem
	x	5x	
x			
x		6x	
	x		
x			
	x		Body of rug
x			
	x		
x			
	x	6x	Hem
	x	5x	
x			
x			
	x	4x	

24 | HIGHLAND CABIN

WARP

8/4 cotton carpet warp

Colors:

Navy Blue (**N**), 272 ends

Moody Blue (**B**), 252 ends

Tan (**T**), 44 ends

Total ends: 568

Sett

24 epi

Width in Reed

23.5 inches

WEFT

Hems

2 strands of Navy 8/4 cotton wound together

Body of Rug

Cotton plaid flannel fabric cut to 1-inch-wide strips

25 | Zigzag

I love weaving Boundweave rugs because the warping is quick and the weaving is slow and Zen-like. I take a lot of pleasure watching the colors and patterns shift as I weave. Boundweave requires a more open sett warp so that the weft materials can easily slide down and cover the warp threads. This makes a very dense and thick rug that will wear like iron and last for years to come. This warp has an open sett of 8 epi. I tore the rags to approximately ¾ inch wide. You will need two contrasting colors of rag material.

Boundweave typically uses a Twill threading and treadling. This variation of Boundweave is called "treadling on opposites." This means that the two weft fabrics are woven on opposite Twill treadlings.

First, you need to decide which of the two fabrics will be the leading, main color. Let's assign it to be called weft A. Then the second fabric will be called weft B. Start by treadling the 1 and 2 treadles and weave weft color A. The opposite will be the 3 and 4 treadles, and it will weave with the B color. Next, we treadle the 2 and 3 Twill and weave color A. This will be followed by treadling 4 and 1 and weaving with the B color. Continue this way by treadling through the Twill sequence and weaving the rag wefts on opposite treadles (see draft).

Many Twill threadings will work for Boundweave. I hope you will be inspired to try others such as M and W Twill, Broken Twill, and Point Twill variations.

Threading

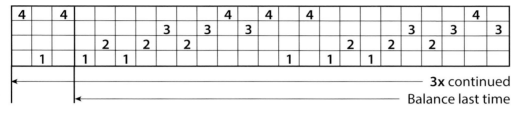

4		4		4		4						4		4		4					
			3		3		3								3		3		3		
						2		2		2								2		2		2
	1		1						1		1		1								1		1

3x ⟶
Balance last time ⟶

Threading (cont.)

4		4						4		4		4							4	
					3		3		3								3		3		3
			2		2		2								2		2		2		
	1		1		1						1		1		1					

⟵ **3x continued** ⟶
⟵ **Balance last time** ⟶

Tie-up

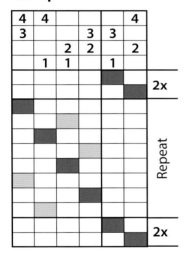

4	4				4
3			3	3	
		2	2		2
	1	1		1	

2x
Repeat
2x

WARP

12/6 Seine Twine, Fiskgarn,
Swedish cotton warp in Brown

Total ends: 201

Sett

8 epi

Note: Sley double in the first two
and last two dents and heddles.

Width in Reed

24.5 inches

WEFT

Beginning and Ending Headers

4 picks of Plain Weave with red
rags

Finish with Damascus edge and
fringe

Body of Rug

Cotton flannel cut to ¾-inch-wide
strips, in colors:

 Red

Beige

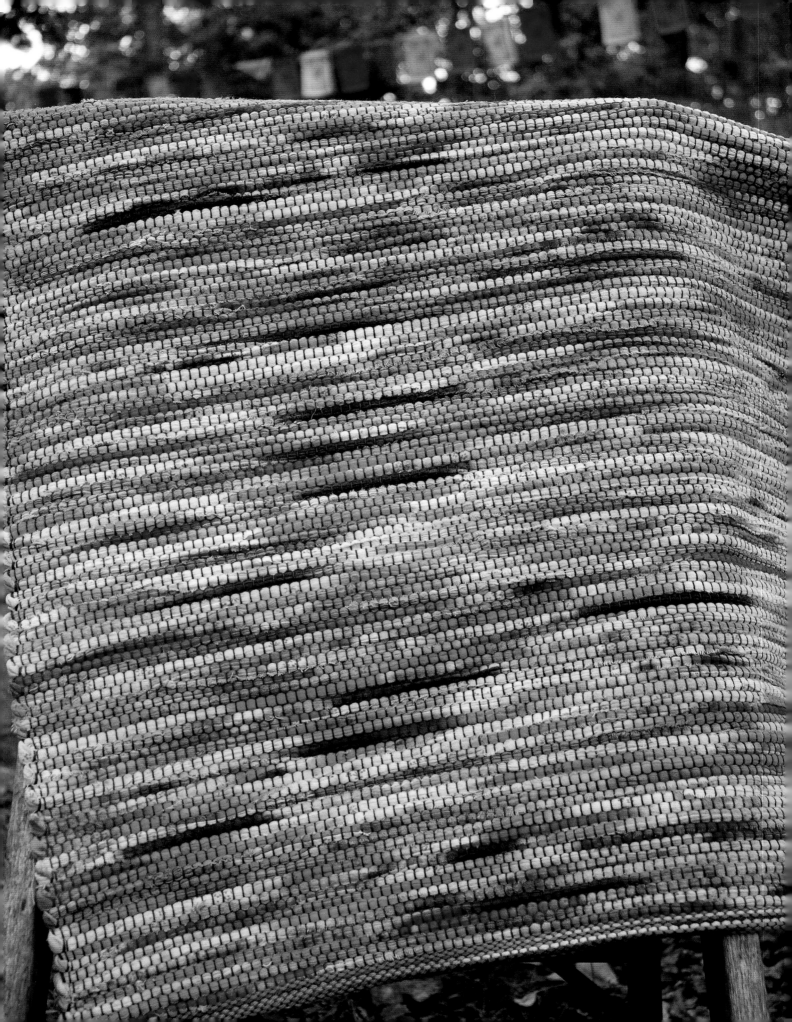

26 | Tie Dye

My wife found a Tulip brand tie-dye kit on sale at our local fabric store. After having a wonderful time tie-dyeing some napkins for our home, Cindy had a lot of dye left over and suggested that I use it up on some of my flannel sheets. I had collected quite a few rather uninteresting light-colored flannel sheets with a small pattern running through them. I was completely uninspired to use them the way they were, so dyeing them was a great idea. I set up a folding table outside on the lawn. The table has a Formica top, so the dye would not hurt the table surface.

We ran the sheets through the washing machine to get them wet and ready to absorb all those bright colors of dye. We scrunched the sheets up on the table to resemble hills and valleys. We then squirted the dye onto the sheets in a very random way. Blue, green, pink, yellow, and many other colors all contributed to making these boring sheets bright and colorful. With rubber-gloved hands, I worked the dye into the folds. I had no idea how it was going to come out, but it didn't really matter because anything would be better than how the sheets looked before dyeing them. When we used up all the dye, we placed the sheets into a white garbage bag and let them sit for 24 hours as the dyeing instructions suggested.

The next day we machine washed the sheets again in a hot, soapy, full wash cycle. There was no bleeding of the colors. They were fabulous tie-dye sheets. I placed them into the dryer to dry. Later I noticed that the original pattern on the sheets was still visible, but faint under all those color splotches. It was certainly interesting to see, but I knew that it wouldn't add any interest to the final patterning of the rug.

I almost regretted having to rip the pretty sheets into strips for rugs, but that was the plan, so I ripped 1½-inch-wide fabric strips. I had a forest green warp left over from another rug project, so I thought I might as well use it. The warp color would complement the colors of the fabric strips. It was a perfect choice.

I decided that I wanted a rolled hem for this rug. I thought hard about what color I should use to weave the hem. It then dawned on me that my wife has a large stash of Sugar 'n Cream cotton yarn and that maybe she would have a variegated skein with the colors of the dyed sheets. I found a skein that worked out to be the perfect match for the rug.

I believe this rug would be a nice addition to a child's bedroom, don't you think?

Threading

4				4				4			
	3				3				3		
		2				2				2	
			1				1				1

Tie-up

	4		
3			
	2		
1			
x		4x	
	x		
	x	5x	Hem
x			
x		6x	
	x		
x			
	x		
x			Body of rug
	x		
x			
	x	6x	
	x		
x		5x	Hem
x			
	x	4x	

WARP

12/6 Seine Twine, Fiskgarn, Swedish cotton warp in Dark Green

Total ends: 196

Sett

8 epi

Note: Double sley the first two and last two dents and heddles.

Width in Reed

24 inches

WEFT

Hems

Multicolored Sugar 'n Cream cotton yarn

Body of Rug

Tie-dyed cotton flannel sheets cut to 1½-inch-wide strips

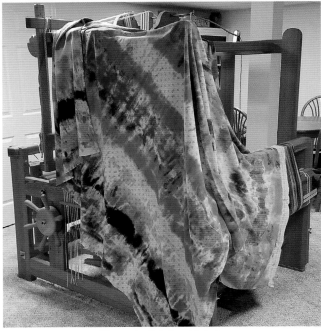

The colorful dyed fabric

27 | Weftovers

Over the years I have woven many rag rugs using old sheets, unwanted old fabric, new fabric, old clothing, and other contributing sources for making rag strips for my rugs. I usually cut or tear the strips ahead of weaving the rug. After tearing the strips to the width I want, I roll them into balls until the day I am ready to weave. I don't always use all the prepared rag strips in one rug, but I don't have the heart to throw the unused and leftover balls of strips away. So the leftover rags get tossed into a basket or two until inspiration moves me to weave a new rug using these leftovers. So ask me, how many baskets of rags do I have? Lots and lots.

The average weaver can accumulate plenty, but when you decide to write a book about rag rugs and want to show many examples of different rugs in your book, well, you end up with a lot of leftovers.

My wife suggested I try to use up some of these leftover balls in just one rug. She proposed that I randomly pick something out of the basket and weave it up, something like the old "hit-or-miss" rugs of the past. These were woven with all the old clothes and worn-out textiles from around the house. What a superb idea, but I just couldn't do it! I started going through all those baskets and picking rags that looked good together, complemented each other. My heart wouldn't let me throw in a hot pink rag strip next to a brown tweed rag. I know, I know, anything can go in those rugs, but it wasn't in me to do that. Besides, I had plenty to choose from and was in no danger of running out, leaving me with a shorter-than-normal rug.

To my thinking, any color is good as long as it is *blue*. So, for this warp, I decided to make a warp with blue and ecru pinstripes. You will see in the draft that there are five pattern areas, each measuring 5 inches in width. The two outside areas and the center area of the rug use wide pinstripes, while the other two areas use finely spaced stripes. Each of the areas measure 5 inches in width, making the rug 25 inches wide in the reed.

Again, when I warp my loom, I like to make a long warp so I can weave several rugs on the same warp. I can change out the rags or even change up the treadling to make a different-looking rug from the others. You'll see this draft again in Pebbly (page 97).

I hope you like what I did with my "weftovers."

Threading

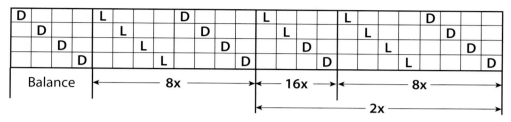

				L				D				L			L				D			
D					L				D				L			L				D			
	D					L				D				D			L				D		
		D					L				D			D				L				D	
			D					L				D			D				L				D

Balance	8x	16x	8x
		2x	

Tie-up

	4
3	
	2
1	

x		
	x	4x
	x	
x		5x
x		
	x	6x
x		
	x	
x		Body of rug
	x	
x		
	x	6x
	x	
x		5x
x		
	x	4x

Hem (top) / Body of rug / Hem (bottom)

WARP

8/4 cotton carpet warp

Colors:

Navy Blue (**D**), 164 ends

Ecru (**L**), 160 ends

Total ends: 324 + 4 for doubled selvedge edges = 328

Sett

12 epi

Note: Sley double in first two and last two dents and heddles.

Width in Reed

27 inches

WEFT

Hem

2 strands of Navy 8/4 cotton wound together

Body of Rug

Leftover rags from previous rugs, all cotton, cut to 1½ inches wide

28 | Step by Step

After our friend Carol passed away, her husband was faced with cleaning out and finding homes for Carol's accumulated stash of yarns, looms, and bolts of unused fabric. When I was offered several bolts of madras fabric, I was quick to say yes.

I first machine washed them several times in hot water to remove any excess dye that might bleed out. Madras is notorious for bleeding. I also machine dried them on hot to again help to set the color. I had two bolts that were very compatible colorwise. The printed fabrics were in shades of rust and browns and neutral colors. I think Carol must have had a plan to use them together but just never got around to doing so. This madras fabric is woven from fine cotton threads, and the weight of the fabric is very light and airy.

I thought for a long time on how I was going to use this beautiful fabric, and then it came to me: because of the lightweight nature of this fabric, I could use it for a clasped weft rug technique.

I warped my loom with 8/4 cotton carpet warp in an asymmetrical design. I chose colors that looked good with the colors of the fabric. One side of the warp is heavier in dark-toned colors while the other half is lighter in color and has a bold red stripe running through it.

I tore the rags at ¾-inch width and wound one color into a ball of rags and the other onto a rug shuttle. After spreading the warp and weaving the hem, I started weaving the rags with the clasped weft technique. The darker, rust-colored rag I wound onto the rug shuttle, which I passed from left to right in the first Plain Weave shed. I placed the lighter-colored ball of rags into an old coffee can on the floor and brought up the end of the rag closer to the selvedge edge on the right side of my loom. When the shuttle reached the right side of the loom, I interlocked the two rag strips and sent the rug shuttle back to the left side, pulling the lighter-colored rag with it. I adjusted the clasped portion to just where I wanted it and then beat the two rags down against the hem. I changed the shed to the opposite Plain Weave shed and repeated the process again: Toss the rug shuttle from left to right, clasp the lighter-colored rag, and then send the shuttle back to the left side of the loom. Adjust the position of the clasped area in the open shed, and when you have it just where you want it, close the shed to lock in the rags and beat it down firmly against the fell. Take a look at the photos to help you see how this is done.

I love the clasped weft technique. It works well for scarves and shawls, placemats, and runners. You are only limited by your imagination.

You do have to remember that you are folding the rag or thread back on itself in the open shed, which makes your weft twice as thick as the original rag or thread. The madras fabric worked out perfectly for this clasped weft rug.

Threading

4			4			4	
	3			3			3
		2			2			2
			1			1			1

Tie-up

	4
3	
	2
1	

x		4x	Hem
	x	5x	
x			
	x	6x	
x			

x			Body of rug
	x		
x			
	x		

x		6x	Hem
	x	5x	
x			
x		4x	
	x		

Color Order

			108	38		Linen
					12	Red Cardinal
50		60				Brown
	36					Black

WARP

8/4 cotton carpet warp

Colors:

Linen, 146 ends

Red Cardinal, 12 ends

Brown, 110 ends

Black, 36 ends

Total ends: 304

Sett

12 epi

Note: Sley double in the first two and last two dents and heddles.

Width in Reed

25 inches

WARP

Hem

2 strands Brown 8/4 cotton wound together

Body of Rug

Madras fabric in two colors, cut to ¾-inch-wide strips

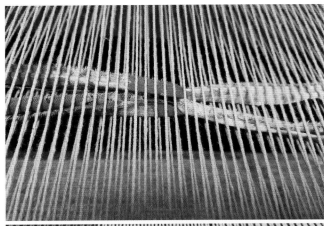

Clasped weft

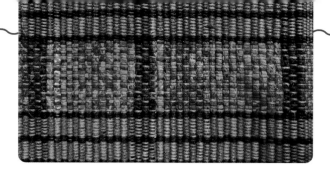

29 | Show Those Stripes

I really like this warp arrangement. It's different from the normal rag rug because it breaks some rules as to how a warp must be put on a loom and woven. It is a little mutinous. Instead of having a warp of 8/4 cotton with a sett of 12 epi, this rug's warp uses 8/4 with setts of 12 *and* 24 epi. That's correct: you have areas in the warp that are closely sleyed and nearly warp faced. Look at the draft and see that there are several colors being used to make what looks like inkle bands. These warp-faced bands alternate with typical stripes of carpet warp at 12 epi. These bands of warp are about 2 inches wide across the warp's width.

I have saved a lot of extra torn strips of rag material. Many of them are from bolts of batik fabric. This fabric is expensive, and I just can't bring myself to throw it out. A little here and a little bit there, and soon you will have saved enough rag strips to weave a new rug.

After I warped the loom, I laid out the different colors of rag strips in piles to see how much I had and counted them. I then put them in some sort of order by color. When I found a sequence that pleased me, I wove that order over and over until I was out of rags. There, I was finished. I now had a handsome new rug from leftover rags.

Since warping is tedious and takes some time, why not warp your loom for two or three rugs? This warp is very accepting of all different kinds of rags. Let's use up those leftover rags and put them to good use.

Warp with alternating setts of 12 epi and 24 epi

Threading

Block A–Warpface Stripe/sleyed 24 epi in 12-dent reed

B			G			B			C			B			G			B	
	B			C			B			G			B			C			B
		B			G			C			B			G			B	
			B			C			G			B			C			B

←— 3x —→   ←— 3x —→   ←— 3x —→

Block B–sleyed 12 epi

T			P			L		
	P			L			T	
		L			T			P
		T			P			L

←————— 2x —————→

Block C–sleyed 12 epi

W			C			D		
	C			D			W	
		D			W			C
		W			C			D

←————— 2x —————→

Tie-up

		4
3		
		2
1		

x		
	x	4x
	x	5x
x		
x		
	x	6x
x		
	x	
x		Body of rug
	x	
x		
	x	6x
	x	
x		5x
x		
	x	4x

Hem (top), *Body of rug* (middle), *Hem* (bottom)

WARP ORDER

A-B-A [C-A-B-A] 3X

WARP

8/4 cotton carpet warp

Colors:

Black (**B**), 128 ends
Copper (**C**), 144 ends
Army Green (**G**), 144 ends
Limestone (**L**), 32 ends
Pear (**P**), 32 ends
Tan (**T**), 32 ends
Dubonnet (**D**), 24 ends
Cranberry (**C**), 24 ends
Wine (**W**), 24 ends

Total ends: 584

Group A: Warp-face Stripe

Sleyed 24 epi in a 12-dent reed

Colors:

B = Black
C = Copper
G = Army Green

Group B

Sleyed 12 epi in a 12-dent reed

Colors:

L = Linen
P = Pear
T = Tan

Group C

Sleyed 12 epi in a 12-dent read

Colors:

D = Dubonnet
C = Cranberry
W = Wine

Sett

12 and 24 epi

Width in Reed

31.25 inches

WEFT

Hem

2 strands (any color from the warp) 8/4 cotton wound together

Body of Rug

Leftover strips of batik cotton fabric 1½ inches wide

Hem

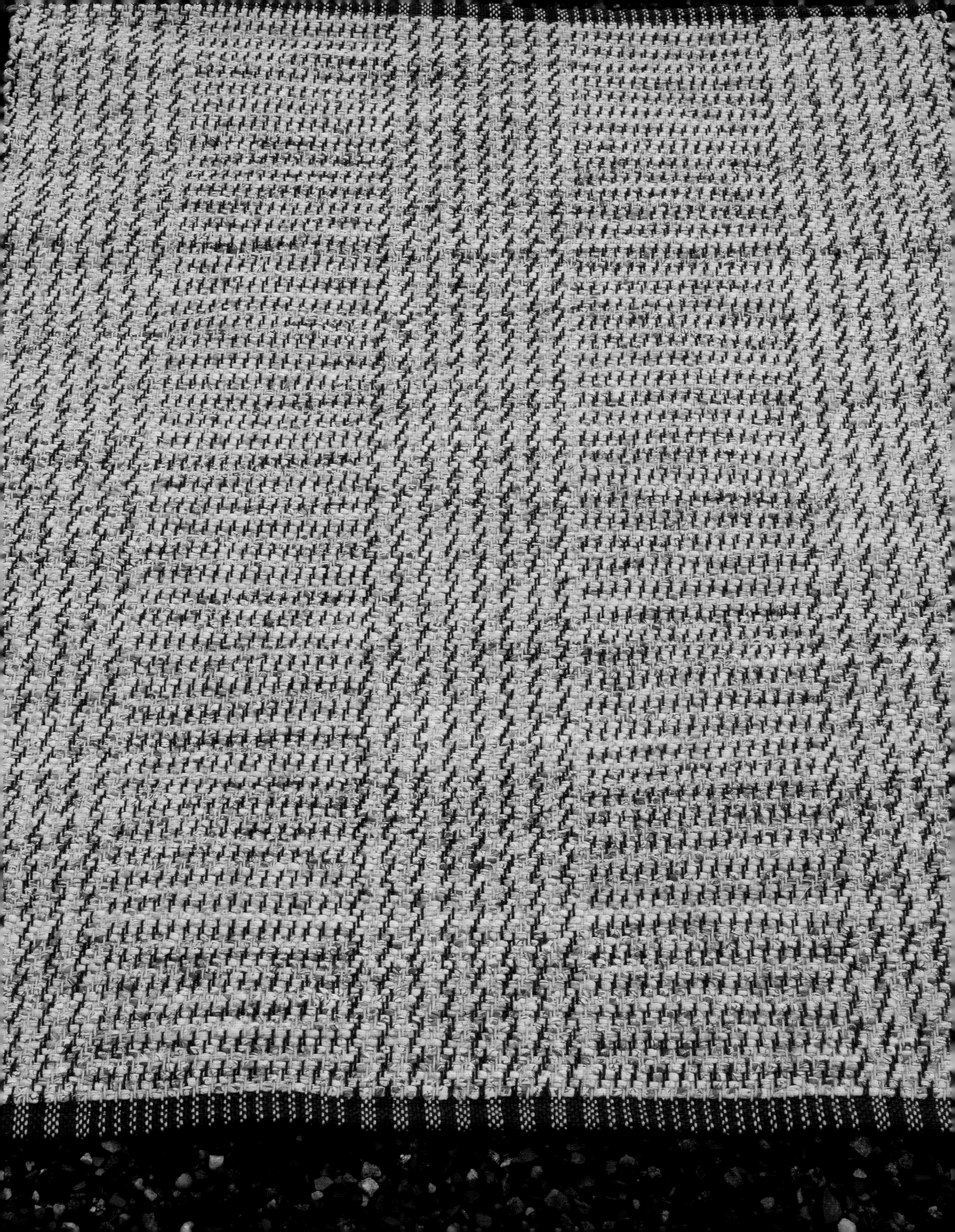

30 | Pebbly

This rug shares the same warp as the Weftovers rug (page 87). It looks totally different, though, because I used an old piece of unloved madras cotton fabric throughout the entire weaving of this rug. I tore the rags to 1½ inches wide. The fabric was several yards long, so I was able to weave with nice long strips of rags. When the rags ran out, I was finished with the rug.

Compare the two rugs. Weftovers was woven as Plain Weave. Pebbly was woven in a simple Twill treadling. You might find it hard to believe that these two rugs were woven on the same warp, but they were. I decided to finish them with a rolled hem.

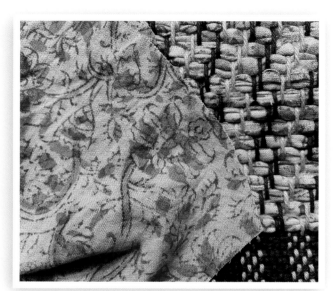

The fabric used for the weft

Threading

D				L			D			L			L			D			
	D				L			D			L			L			D		
		D				L			D			L			L			D	
			D				L			D			D			L			D

Balance	← 8x →	← 16x →	← 8x →

← 2x →

Tie-up

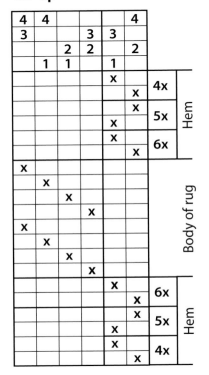

4	4				4
3			3	3	
		2	2		2
	1	1		1	

Hem
				x		4x
					x	
					x	5x
				x		
				x		6x
					x	

Body of rug
x			
	x		
		x	
			x
x			
	x		
		x	
			x

Hem
				x		6x
					x	
					x	5x
				x		
				x		4x
					x	

WARP

8/4 cotton carpet warp

Colors:

Navy Blue (**D**), 164 ends

Ecru (**L**), 160 ends

Total ends: 324 + 4 for doubled selvedge = 328

Sett

12 epi

Note: Sley doubled in first two and last two dents and heddles.

Width in Reed

27 inches

WEFT

Hems

2 strands of Navy 8/4 cotton wound together

Body of Rug

Cotton madras print fabric cut to 1½-inch-wide strips

Rag Rug Weaving Basics

LOOM AND OTHER TOOLS

When weaving rag rugs—or any other heavy textile—you need to be mindful of the fact that you are asking oversized materials to be tightly interwoven to make a solid, hard-wearing item. Rag rugs need to be woven on sturdy looms that will withstand heavy beating; much of the other equipment that you use also needs to be extra strong to handle the challenge of a rag rug. Let's take a look at all the things you will need to make a great rag rug.

Loom

It's easy to get excited about weaving a rag rug and forget to make sure you have a suitable loom to weave it on. Your loom needs to be heavy, sturdy, and very strong. When looking over a loom, make sure that the frame is made of thick and heavy timbers, with tight joints where the pieces come together. This will add to the overall strength.

Most floor looms are fine to weave a rag rug on; the heavier the loom, the better the final results. A portable floor loom that can fold up for easier moving is not a good choice for weaving rugs. Each spot on the loom that folds is a weak spot, and every weak spot compromises the overall sturdiness of the loom. Smaller portable looms and tabletop looms will work for other types of rag weaving (such as rag placemats, table runners, and lightweight textiles such as Japanese sakiori fabric), but for a rug you really want a solidly built floor loom.

Before you start your rug, go over the loom and tighten the nuts and bolts or tap in the wedges that hold the frame together.

Weighting the beater of your loom is a great trick to help you beat the rags into the web of your rug. There are numerous ways to do this, but the one that I think works the best is to simply attach a heavy steel bar to the underside of the beater. I went to a local welding shop and told the owner what my intentions were, and they fixed me up with a piece of steel that was about ⅜ inch thick and 2½ inches wide. They cut this piece to a length that just fit between the uprights of the beater and drilled holes several inches apart down the length of the bar. All I had to do was screw the bar to the beater. The steel bar added about 10 pounds to the beater. At first I was concerned that the added weight would have to be removed when I wasn't weaving rugs, but I got used to the weight of the beater, and for textiles and fabrics that require a lighter beat, I simply pull my punches and don't beat as hard.

You may want to ask your loom manufacturer whether they offer a weighted beater for the loom. If you can order the weights directly from the manufacturer, it could save you a lot of time.

Another good way to prep your loom for the heavy work of rug making is to brace the front uprights to prevent the loom from sliding forward as you beat. To do this, simply cut two pieces of heavy wood to a length that allows you to place them between the front uprights

Brace your loom with wood blocks

A steel bar for weighting the beater

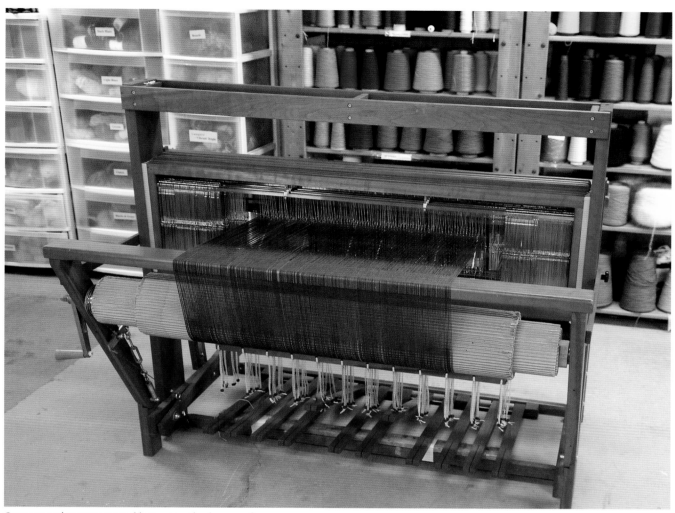

Corrugated paper wound between the layers of warp

and an outside wall of your weaving studio. They should be about 27–30 inches long so as to give you enough space to place your bench between the wall and the loom. Make sure there is a thick and tall baseboard on the outside wall—or, even better, brace your loom against a concrete block wall. You don't want to drive the supports through the wall!

When selecting a loom to weave rag rugs, you also want to think about the shedding action. There are three types of looms to consider. Jack looms have a shedding system that raises the shafts. There are also counterbalance looms and countermarch looms, in which the shafts move in opposite directions. The two latter types of looms are generally preferred by rug weavers the world over because of the increased shed opening. This makes it easier to work with large shuttles wound with bulky materials. With the jack loom, the warp threads lie on the shuttle race of the beater and are at their lowest position when the shed is

being opened. The warp needs to be kept tight for rag rug weaving, but if it is too tight, it can be difficult to achieve a shed that allows for easy weaving. If you are weaving on a jack loom, you might need to decrease the tension on the warp slightly to get a great shed. With the counterbalance or countermarch loom, the tight warp threads pass through the loom's reed above the shuttle race at a distance about a third of the height of the reed. The warp moves both up and down, creating a larger shed than can be achieved on a jack loom, where the warp only goes up.

The counterbalance loom works well as a two- or four-shaft loom, but the countermarch loom, with its more complex tie-up, can easily weave as an eight-, ten-, sixteen-, or twenty-shaft loom. However, there are very few instances in weaving rag rugs when an eight-shaft loom is required. Warp-face rep weave is an exception, as with this type of weaving the designs become crisper and more complex the more shafts you use.

A sectional warp beam

The majority of rag rugs can be woven on four or fewer shafts; many are woven as a simple Plain Weave.

Another important consideration is the type of heddle on your loom. Heddles with small eyes are more difficult to thread and also present a chafing problem for thicker warp threads. Inserted eye heddles and nylon heddles are good choices for rug weaving, as they allow the warp threads to pass through more easily. The nylon heddles are very flexible and may be slightly slower to thread than the wire heddles with the inserted eye. I prefer the inserted eye heddles on a shaft with a solid frame and the nylon heddles on Scandinavian-style looms that have wooden heddle bars only on the top and bottom of the shaft.

The loom will have either a flat warp beam or a sectional warp beam (easily recognized by the wooden or metal pins that extend outward from the beam and divide the beam into one- or two-inch sections). The flat warp beam is more common. When you wind the warp onto this beam, you will need to separate the layers with heavy paper, single-face corrugated paper, or the tried-and-true method used for centuries, wooden slats. The wooden slats are inserted into the warp with each

turn of the beam. Several slats per turn is not excessive, as this helps to keep the warp under even tension. If you are using heavy paper or corrugated paper, feed it into the warp as you wind the warp onto the warp beam to separate the layers. Without the wooden slats or paper, the warp will collapse under the tension put on it when weaving.

The sectional warp beam, with its dividers, doesn't require paper or slats because the pegs extending out from the warp beam support the warp threads, preventing them from spreading and collapsing under the warp's tension. With this kind of warp beam, the warp is wound one section at a time.

Shuttles

The rag rug weaver's shuttles are larger than the boat shuttles used for fabric weaving. They need to be able to hold large amounts of rags so that the weaver can weave several inches of the rug before having to join a new end. Rag shuttles remind me of a catamaran boat: They have two smoothly finished side boards turned on end and held together with two or three crosspieces.

Rag shuttle

Ski shuttle

Rug shuttle

The space between the side boards measures between 1½ and 2 inches. This allows you to wind several yards of rags flatly, without folding or twisting, around the middle of the shuttle.

Ski shuttles resemble a ski with two turned-up ends. A board attached perpendicularly to the flat side of the ski holds the rags. With each of these shuttles, you need to wind the rags onto the shuttle by hand and then unwind the rags by a few turns before you throw the shuttle. The process may seem very awkward at first, but remember that rag rugs weave up very quickly.

In the beginning and ending portion of each rag rug, a heading needs to be woven to secure the rags. This is usually woven with a conventional boat shuttle.

Temple

This tool is known by several names—"temple," "tenterhook," and "stretcher"—and is a device that keeps the selvedges from pulling in. The temple is made of wood or metal and slides much like a slide rule to adjust to several weaving widths. At the ends there are sharp stainless-steel teeth that, when inserted into the meaty part of the rug, help to prevent the edges from naturally pulling in. Place the temple into the rug as soon as possible, adjusting it to the width of the warp as it is in the reed. As you weave your rug, move the temple every 1½ to 2 inches for the length of the rug. This doesn't prevent the rug from ultimately drawing in but does keep it pulled out to the weaving width when the beater and reed strike the fell of your rug.

Wood and metal temples

Rotary cutter and cutting mat

Scissors, Rag Cutters, and Rotary Cutters

Treat yourself to a great pair of scissors that are made of good-quality materials. Gingher and Fisker, as well as some other manufacturers, are good choices to pick for your weaving studio. Keep them away from the kitchen drawer, craft drawer, and, most of all, other members of the family, who might mistake them for just another pair of scissors and use them for cutting paper, removing price tags, or cutting up chicken pieces. Mark them somehow as yours. If and when they do get dull, you can sharpen them.

For cutting long lengths of rags there is nothing better than a rag cutting machine or a rotary cutter with a guide and self-healing cutting mat. The rag cutting machine has been used for years and is a staple among rug hookers, who use it for cutting narrow strips of wool. An adjustable guide lets you cut strips of any width you like. The machine clamps to a table or workbench and works very much like a pasta machine. A metal roller holds the fabric down and pushes it onto a sharp rotating cutting blade; as you turn the handle, the fabric is drawn in and cut to the desired width, and the finished rag strips come out the other end. You simply cut the

Rag cutting machine

rags one strip at a time for as many strips as you need or until the fabric is completely cut into strips.

A handheld rotary cutter is another good choice for cutting your rags. It looks much like a small pizza cutter but with an extremely sharp cutting edge that needs to be respected. You will have best results with the rotary cutter if you combine it with a cutting mat and a clear plastic guide.

The cutting mat is marked off with ruled measurements on four sides. Simply place the mat on a stable surface and lay your fabric on it. Place the clear plastic guide on top of the fabric at the spot where you want to make the cut and run the rotary cutter along the guide's edge, pressing firmly to go through the fabric. You can fold the fabric to a size that's more manageable and then cut through several layers at once. Blades for the rotary cutter are interchangeable, so when a blade gets dull, you can simply replace it.

Sewing Machine

In years past, rug makers would sit and sew the cut strips of fabric together by hand. This was a common practice and a good way to pass the time in the evening while listening to the radio. Sometimes people would get together as a social activity and cut and sew rags and catch up with the local gossip. Many hours were spent sewing small fabric strips together by hand. The invention of the sewing machine changed the lives of thousands of households—including those of rag rug weavers. Today's rag rug weaver doesn't need to have the fanciest sewing machine. A machine that will do a few basic functions such as a straight stitch and zigzag stitch is all you need for most aspects of rag rug weaving. If you choose to do a machine-stitched hem, then you will need a heavy-duty sewing machine that can sew through several layers of bulky material.

Washing Machine and Iron

It may seem funny to include a washing machine and an iron on the list of tools for weaving a rag rug, but in fact they are both essential tools. The washing machine is important for preparing the fabric to be woven into the rug—new fabric needs to be washed to remove the finish and preshrink it before it's cut up and incorporated into a rug. You'll need the iron in the finishing process to press a neat hem and to block the rug so it lies flat on the floor. Some people also use an iron in preparing the rags, folding in the cut edges and steam pressing them in place. This makes a neat and clean-looking rug but is so time consuming that many people choose not to press their rags. The iron is such an essential tool that it is worth investing in a good-quality professional steam iron that's rather heavy.

Tape Measure

Get a sturdy tape measure that doesn't stretch. You'll want one that measures up to 120 inches; a shorter tape measure will work just fine, but for measuring long lengths, you will love not having to measure to a certain length and then shift the tape and measure some more.

Pins, T-Pins, and Tapestry Needles

These are just little things, but I promise you will be using all of them all the time. If you don't already have these items among your sewing notions, please go out and buy them.

MATERIALS

The materials used to weave a rag rug can be as diverse as the people who weave them. For their first rag rug, many weavers often choose to weave with traditional materials such as a cotton warp and a weft of cotton rags. Environmentally conscious weavers may choose to use only organic cotton warp threads and never a thread that is petroleum based; for weft, they use recycled rags instead of new fabric. Some weavers take the recycling movement to a new level, using grocery bags, newspaper sleeves, washed garbage bags, old nylon stockings, or the legs of pantyhose for outdoor mats to wipe your feet on. An acrylic or nylon warp with these unconventional rags makes them easy to wash and nearly indestructible.

When choosing the materials for your rag rug, be sure to use well-made and strong warp threads and weft materials that can be washed and will hold up to wear. A well-woven rag rug should last for years—even decades.

Let's take a look at the different options of materials for your warp and weft.

Warp Threads

COTTON THREAD

Cotton threads are some of the most popular and easiest threads to work with, especially if this is your first rag rug. Good-quality cotton rug warp comes in several thread sizes and prepackaged quantities. The most widely used cotton thread is size 8/4 carpet warp, which can be found in dozens of colors. Also available is a line of 8/4 thread that is 50% cotton and 50% polyester. The addition of polyester helps the thread stand up to multiple washings without the fringe disintegrating. Pure cotton doesn't hold up nearly as well in a fringed rug; its short staple length soon unravels and comes apart after multiple washings, leaving you with just the knots at the rug's edge. For weavers who like to use 100% cotton for their warps, a rolled hem is a sensible alternative to a fringe that may not last through lots of washings.

Two more great choices for cotton warp for rag rugs are Seine Twine and Fishgarn. Seine Twine is composed of many strands of plied cotton threads. It is heavy and very, very strong, making it ideal for rug weaving of all kinds. Seine Twine is available only in natural-colored cotton, however. If your plan is to weave a rug that is mostly weft faced and the warp thread is covered or doesn't play a major role in the design, then Seine Twine may be perfect for you. If your design requires a colored warp, another material may be a better choice. Many good weaving supply stores carry Seine Twine; you can also look for it at your local hardware store (masons use cotton twine for plumb lines to keep brick walls straight, and gardeners will use it for laying out straight rows).

Fishgarn, like Seine Twine, is made up of multiple strands of plied cotton thread. This yarn is imported from Scandinavia, and its name means "fish yarn." When you look closely at a piece of Fishgarn, you can see that it resembles the thread used to make fishing nets. Fishgarn comes in a great number of sizes. Some weaving shops carry Fishgarn in a limited number of colors. Though the dyed yarn is noticeably more expensive than natural cotton yarn, it may be worth it to you to have the colored yarn in the rug's design and in the fringe.

Mop cotton is another material that can be used for rug warp. When you hear "mop cotton," most likely the stuff on the end of a mop (like the kinds that school custodians use for cleaning hallways and classroom floors) comes to mind. That type of mop cotton is soft spun and best used in rugs as weft. The mop cotton that I like to use for warp is more tightly spun and is made by plying many strands of finer cotton thread together to create a heavy cotton cord. This type of mop cotton also is available in many colors. It has approximately 400–450 yards to the pound, so, as you can see, it is quite heavy and makes a good warp yarn.

Mercerized cotton, or perle cotton, is another, often-overlooked option for warp. It has a shiny finish that is the effect of an alkali solution that polishes the thread. Perle cotton is readily available in heavier-weight threads such as 3/2 and 5/2 cotton and is dyed to dozens of beautiful colors. When a design such as rep weave calls for a rug to be warp faced or warp emphasized, I

Cotton carpet warp

will often turn to perle cotton for my warp. Perle cotton is very strong and can easily take the abrasion that's put on the threads in weaving warp faced.

LINEN THREAD

Linen thread is very strong and hard wearing, an excellent choice for rag rugs. Because linen is also very dense, a rug woven with a linen warp (or, for that matter, with a linen warp and linen rag weft) will lie flat on the floor and will shift around less than rugs made with less dense materials. One important characteristic of linen thread to keep in mind is that it has little to no elasticity; it doesn't give or spring back into position if knocked with your shuttle. Because of this, you need to make sure your warp threads are evenly tensioned when working with linen. This is more easily achieved when weaving on a floor loom, especially a deep (long from the front to the back) countermarch or counterbalance loom. Rug linen is available in its natural color of gray-brown, which makes it a nice neutral base for any color of rags that you wish to weave into it. The standard sizes for rug linen are 8/2, 8/3, 8/4, and 8/5. The second number refers to the number of plies to the thread, so the larger this number is, the thicker the thread. The first number indicates the size of the individual thread. This numbering system is standard in the textile industry and

Heavy mop cotton

Seine Twine and linen rug warp

is used to identify many weaving threads. Treat yourself to a linen warp sometime and compare for yourself the differences between linen and cotton warp.

WOOL YARN

Rag rug weavers rarely use wool for rug warp. Somehow this fiber just gets overlooked. But it doesn't need to be! I personally love to combine wool rags with a wool warp that is well spun and plied. Over time and with use, the wool warp threads bind with the woolen rags in a process known as felting. Look for a 3- or 4-ply wool that is tightly spun without a lot of elasticity. You need a yarn that is rough or even hairy. Never use a knitting yarn. Knitting yarns are made from varieties of sheep that provide soft wool, and the yarns are spun with a gentle twist, giving the yarn some stretch when you pull on it. Wool rug warp can be found in a variety of colors as well as the natural colors of sheep wool; you can also dye the natural wool, even blacks, grays, and browns, which will give you deep, rich colors, adding lots of beauty and interest to your rugs. Imagine weaving strips of heather wool fabric into a gray tweed warp. Fantastic!

SYNTHETIC YARN

I have to admit that I don't associate the old timey charm of a rag rug with synthetic materials. But why not? These yarns were developed to make our lives more comfortable and washing and ironing less labor intensive. Acrylic, nylon, and polyester yarns and threads can be used as warp yarns, with the exception of those acrylic yarns that are meant to be knitting yarns. Ask your weaving store owner if they carry an acrylic rug warp about the size of 8/4 cotton. This will be a sturdy thread that can take the stress of weaving and beating the rags back into the web. As mentioned earlier, you can buy polyester-cotton-blend 8/4 carpet warp, which comes in a variety of colors. The advantage of using synthetics for your warp is in the finishing of the rug. A fringe made from synthetic fibers will hold up well to wear and washing.

Weft Fabrics

When thinking about the rags for your rug, you have a lot of choices. You can recycle fabric by cutting up unwanted clothing, sheets, and blankets, just as the weavers did in the past. Or you can buy new fabric for options that go far beyond what you can get from repurposing old and unwanted clothes. When you go into a large fabric store, it is sometimes overwhelming. There are so many types of fabric to choose from, and the selection of colors is vast. Don't be afraid to ask for help (although once you've read this chapter, you may have

Tightly spun wool warp

more insight into which fabrics would be best for a rag rug than many fabric store employees).

Look around the store and start by eliminating the fabrics you don't want. You will quickly get a feel for it. Burlap, bridal veiling with hand-sewn pearls, leatherette, and upholstery fabrics are not first on my list either. Although you could use any of these materials for weaving a rag rug, it's unlikely that you would want to cut them into strips and weave them into a warp. But don't dismiss wild and crazy prints. What you might find hideous just may turn out to be a wonderful choice when crunched down into a rug. I once found a printed cotton fabric showing a map of the world with each country in a different color. *Who would want this and how would you use it?* I thought. But the price was perfect at two dollars a yard, and I had a coupon that I could use. To my surprise, the material wove up into a spectacular rag rug. The prints with cartoon superheroes and holiday themes are also good.

Even before you think of color or design, you need to think about what type of fabric you want to use—cotton, linen, wool, or something else. Let's break this down to some of the best fabric options to try for rag rugs.

COTTON AND COTTON BLENDS

Solid-color cottons and cotton prints are always good. With solid-color fabric, both sides of the fabric are fully saturated with the color, and you don't have to worry about one side of the fabric being lighter than the other. With cotton prints, the pattern is pressed onto the fabric and the dye bleeds through to the back, leaving a fainter version of what the front of the fabric looks like. Try to look for prints with good color saturation on the reverse side so you don't feel the need to fold the cut strips to hide the lighter side of the fabric. If the fabric you're weaving with is much lighter on the reverse side and you make no attempt to hide the lighter side, the rag strip will twist and both sides will appear within the same row of the woven rug. The result is a mottled effect—which can be quite beautiful, if that's the look you're going for.

There are some patterned cottons that are the same on both sides. Batiks usually have colorful and bold patterns and look the same on both sides. They are more expensive than printed cottons but well worth the extra cost when you see how easy they are to weave. Gingham and plaid patterned fabrics are woven with different colors of thread in the warp and weft; the "homespun" aisle will have old timey and country-style patterns woven from dyed threads. These types of fabric will look the same, or similar, on both sides.

Also consider cotton fabrics in other textures. Flannels are wonderful to use as rags, and the finished rug will feel delightful under your feet. The soft, luxurious feel of flannel makes these rag rugs the perfect choice to put beside your bed and to step onto first thing in the morning. Both denim and corduroy hold up to lots of wear. Rugs woven from denim and corduroy can be placed in high-traffic areas where they are stepped on regularly and pick up a lot of dirt. Their durability makes them also easy to wash and vacuum. Rag rugs woven from the legs of denim jeans are beautiful because of the different degrees of wear on the fabric. There may be dozens of shades of indigo in just one rug woven from old worn jeans. When you spiral cut the legs of a pair of blue jeans, the side seams add textural interest and a rustic look to the rug.

COTTON KNITS

Knitted cotton fabrics can also be used in rag rugs—and, of course, they come with their own advantages and challenges. A knitted material will stretch more than a woven fabric, so working with knits presents some challenges. To prevent excessive draw-in as you weave your rug, pull hard on the rag strip and stretch it as you wind the shuttle. By stretching the fabric out of shape, you help to guarantee that it won't draw back to its original form. Look to see how much thinner the rag is now that you pulled on it. To keep with tradition of using a thicker weft to weave a heavy rug, you might want to cut the knit fabric twice as wide as you would a woven fabric strip.

A rag rug is a marvelous way to use up a collection of old T-shirts. When you think about the color of the shirt itself and then add the printed graphics on top, you can't help but have a handsome strip of rag. You can mix lots of colors from dozens of different T-shirts or go with a theme. Try using the old T-shirts collected from just one source, such as your child's soccer team. This way you will get a lot of material that's already prewashed and all in the same color theme.

When weaving a rug with knits, keep to only knit fabric. Do not mix knits with woven strips. By mixing the two, you risk ending up with a rug that may buckle and not lie flat on the floor. You may think that all that preshrinking of the fabric from washing and all the pulling and stretching would stabilize the rag strips. Well, it might work and you might get lucky—but personally, I don't take the risk. Remember to weave "wovens with wovens and knits with knits. Never mix them together, or they will give you fits."

LINEN FABRIC

Linen is a dense, heavy fabric; rugs woven from it are heavy, lie flat on the floor, and don't shift around as easily as rugs from other materials. It is expensive, however, requiring you to get creative. Look for sales or use those discount coupons from national chain stores and buy the whole bolt. I like using suit-weight linen fabric for my rag rugs, but finding it in colors has proved to be quite a challenge. I will buy an entire bolt of natural-color linen and then dye the fabric myself; the easiest way to do this is to dye the fabric and then cut the rag strips. (Please, never the other way round. You will end up with a ball of tangled rag strips.) Because of the high cost of linen and its limited selections in stores, you might want to try asking your friends and relatives if they have any old linen tablecloths that they don't want anymore. Because of our relaxed habits of entertaining these days, few people are using linen tablecloths and napkins. You may be surprised at how many of your friends are storing old wedding presents in their attics and are only too happy to give you sets of never-used tablecloths. Just please promise me you will never cut up antique hand-woven linens. Those beautiful old handspun and hand-woven linens with indigo blue or brown checks should be given respect and placed into the hands of people who will truly love them. Send them to me! Another good source for linen material is used clothing stores such as Salvation Army and Goodwill. Sometimes people will donate linen shirts, skirts, and dresses because they don't want to be bothered with ironing them. Goody for you, though. It's a cheap way to acquire a collection of linen rags.

WOOL AND WOOL BLENDS

Weaving with wool or any protein-based fiber is pure joy. Protein-based fiber refers to any fiber that origi-nated from an animal. Other fabrics that are protein based include mohair, camel hair, alpaca, and silk. All of these fabrics are luxury items and expensive to buy as on-the-bolt material, so if you want to use wool, you'll likely want to start gathering secondhand wool fabric. Putting together a collection of wool rags from old clothing takes some time. Start by looking at thrift stores, yard sales, church sales, and community out-reach shops for jackets, coats, skirts, and blankets that you can take apart and cut into rag strips. The strips will be short in length, but this gives you the opportunity to mix colors. Try placing dark colors next to lighter colors and warm colors alternating with cool colors for a pleasing hit-or-miss look to your rug. Wool and protein-based fabrics (even if they contain a small percentage of nylon or other synthetic) are some of the easiest to dye. Even darker fabrics such as charcoal and dark browns can be overdyed to get deep, rich colors; these types of colors are more challenging to achieve when starting with natural white. If you buy new fabric to cut into rag strips, look for medium to heavy suit-weight or coat-weight fabric. These weave into a plush-feeling rug. Your feet will thank you for caring. Start by looking at your local fabric stores, and don't forget to watch for those discount coupons offered by some of the chains. I have used online stores as well and found them to be wonderful for their prices, shipping costs, and delivery times.

OTHER MATERIALS

There are some very nice synthetic fabrics on the market that make wonderful rags. Polar fleece, because of its remarkable softness and the way it washes so easily, is a good choice for rag rug strips. It comes in lots of pretty colors and is reasonably priced. You could buy enough for a bedspread plus enough to weave into matching rugs for the sides of the bed. I personally steer clear of rayons and nylons because of their slippery nature. When you weave a rag rug with rayon or nylon, the rug tends to slide around on the floor and becomes a hazard to walk on. A box full of satin binding may at first seem like a gift—already precut and ready to weave. But the resulting rug will be slick and may cause you to fall if you don't put a skid-proof mat under the rug.

The "loopers" that are made from sock tops and sold for making pot holders are also a nice alternative to weaving with fabric strips. By interlocking the loopers end to end, you can make a long continuous length of weft material.

For a rag rug that needs to be really hard wearing and take a lot of washings, try using nylon stockings, panty-hose, and tights. These come in lots of shades of natural skin tones as well as colors such as green, blue, purple, red, and white. They are made of nylon, so they would be slippery and dangerous on a tile floor, but for a rug to put outside on a wooden deck, they would be just fine.

You can even try weaving with recycled plastic bags from the grocery store. Spiral-cut the bags into long strips and weave away! This type of rug is best cleaned by hosing it off and leaving it outside to dry.

These are just a few suggestions of the materials you can try—there are many possibilities, and people are always thinking of new ones. Once I was attending a craft show in Washington, DC, and came across a weaver with the most beautiful rag rugs. The rugs had a textured appearance and soft colors that were very appealing. When I explained that I was also a weaver and was wondering about her weft materials, the weaver generously divulged her secret: She uses old wool sweaters that she picks up at yard sales and consignment stores and from friends and relatives who are cleaning out their winter clothes. She washes and dries them in the dryer until they are half their original size; with the sweaters felted and shrunk up tightly, she can cut them into strips and weave with them just the way they are. They are so tightly felted that the strips simply can't unravel.

You don't need to spend a lot of money on your first rag rug endeavor. Remember, the first rag rugs were woven by frugal people who made their own rugs and carpeting from old, worn-out clothing. Don't overthink it—just jump in and weave a rug!

HOW MUCH FABRIC DO I NEED FOR A RAG RUG?

Calculating the amount of warp you need is really quite straightforward. You determine the sett, or number of ends per inch (epi), that corresponds to the type of warp you are using; then multiply that by the width and length you intend to make the rug (see page 8 for more information on calculating warp).

Calculating the amount of weft fabric you will be using is another story. There is no easy formula, and it can be difficult to figure out how much of a particular fabric you need to make a rug.

Books on the weaving of rag rugs always give the same answer: To weave a rag rug approximately 3 feet by 5 feet, you need about 5–6 pounds of rags. This was an answer but still not a very useful one. I could just imagine myself going into a national fabric chain store with a baby scale under my arm, plopping it on the counter, and then asking the salesperson to just keep unwinding the bolt until we reached 6 pounds. Yeah, right!

I decided to do a little experimenting. I bought one yard each of several different fabrics, cut them into 1½-inch-wide strips, and then wove them into a warp of 8/4 cotton carpet warp set at 12 ends per inch, 12 inches wide in the reed. This way, I could see exactly how much coverage I could get from my one yard of each of the fabrics. At last, I would get a definitive answer to how much fabric it would take to weave a square foot of a rag rug!

The answer is that there is no definitive answer. On average, one yard of apparel-weight cotton fabric or quilters' cotton will yield about one square foot of a rag rug (most times it took a little less than a yard of fabric to weave a square foot, so buying a full yard of fabric was like having insurance). But the story changes with heavier fabrics like denim, corduroy, and coat-weight wool. When I wove these fabrics, I cut the strips to a width of 1 inch because the fabrics were so much heavier and thicker. These samples often wove to 16–18 inches. So what I found was that heavier-weight fabrics require much less yardage to cover a square foot.

Use my discoveries as a preliminary guide, but when in doubt, always weave a sample using a yard of the fabric that you are planning to use. ✳

PREPARING THE RAGS

Now that you've selected your fabric—whether it's a new off-bolt cotton print, a bag of old wool skirts from a thrift store, or a collection of linen tablecloths donated by friends—and calculated how much you'll need, it's time to prepare it for being woven into the rug.

Washing the Fabric

If you're using new fabric, the first step is to wash it to remove the finish that's placed on it at the mill. (Just walk into a fabric store and take a deep breath. You can smell the finish!) Washing and drying the fabric also makes cutting and tearing the fabric much easier and preshrinks the fabric so you don't experience as much shrinkage with the first washing of the rug. In addition, beating is easier with prewashed rags. I either line dry the fabric or put it into the dryer, but I do not use fabric softener or dryer sheets, which just put another layer of chemicals on the surface of the fabric.

If you are planning on weaving a wool rag rug, it's advisable to felt the fabric. Take the length of new fabric (or recycled wool from clothing) and wash it on a regular cycle with hot water and a cold rinse to tighten it up and shrink it. Today high-efficiency washing machines with front-end loading to conserve water usage are popular; although these machines do a marvelous job with the family clothes, they tend not to be the best for felting wool. If you are going to work with wool rags, you might want to use a top loader (if you or a friend has one—or go to a laundromat). These machines work great for felting wool rags.

Now for a word of caution from your author: Wash your rags before you cut them! Without thinking, I once placed a large amount of precut rag strips, each several yards long, into the washer to remove the finish. As the rag strips washed, they entangled themselves around the agitator. This is a mess that I hope you never have to deal with. If you do come across some precut rags (such as factory ends) and want to wash them, place them in a laundry bag that closes at one end. You will be so glad you did.

Preparing Purchased Fabric

Now it's time to cut or tear the strips. This is a dusty job, so do it in a large room with lots of space or even outside. If you are sensitive to this sort of work, you should wear a dust mask to protect your lungs.

I like tearing my fabric strips. It's quick and easy, though it does have some drawbacks. You often end up with a frayed edge and lots of loose threads to deal with. I don't mind this at all—actually, I like the look. After all, it is a rag rug! The straggling loose threads can be pulled off as you wind the strips of fabric onto the shuttle.

Tear the strips with the length of the fabric to get the longest fabric strips you can. Start by making cuts about 4–5 inches deep along one cut end of your fabric at the width that you want your strips to be (about 1½ inches for quilting cotton, shirt-weight fabric, and flannel; 1 inch for denim and wool). I make a cardboard template to help maintain even widths. You can also just measure it out with a tape measure or yardstick.

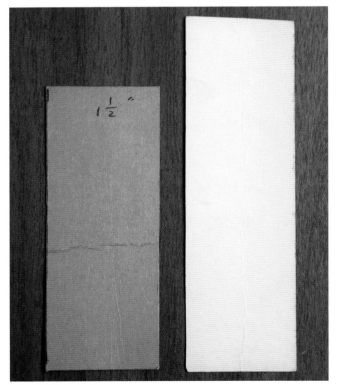

Templates

Then simply grab hold of the fabric strip that your deep cut started and tear down the length of your fabric.

If you precut all the deep cuts into the fabric, you can recruit a friend to help, and you two will have the time of your lives. Start by holding onto the first strip, and let your friend grab the next strip. You then take the next strip and your friend the next. Keep alternating the strips between you, and then start pulling against each other in opposite directions. It's a lot like having a tug of war. Giggles and laughter are often experienced by the participants.

Not all fabrics will tear easily. Wool, linen, and Twill weaves are a challenge and may not tear at all. You will then need to resort to a pair of scissors or rug cutter.

To cut your fabric, you obviously need a very sharp pair of scissors or a cutter. Cut along the length of the fabric to your desired width. If you get a little off in your measurement, it is not the end of the world. It will all even out in the weaving.

I like using a rotary cutter with a cutting mat and guide to cut my strips. If your fabric is not too long—say, just a few yards long—you can fold it into several layers and lay the fabric onto the mat. Then place the clear Lucite guide on top of the fabric and, using your rotary cutter, slice through all the layers at once, creating a nice long strip of fabric.

I have also used a fabric cutting machine that is often used to cut wool fabric for hooked rugs. This cutter attaches to a work table and has a guide that you can adjust to the width of the strips you want. Place the fabric on the tray of the cutter, with the edge along the guide. Turn the handle to draw the fabric into the cutter; the resulting cut strip comes out the other end. It's somewhat like a pasta machine, though it only does one strip at a time.

After the fabric strips are cut or torn, I like to taper the ends by making a diagonal cut that's about 4–5 inches long on each end. This way, as you are weaving and your strip comes to the end, you can easily overlap the new strip over the old one and beat it down into place without any sign of a join (unless the new strip is a different color).

If you are working with shorter lengths of fabric (say, 2 yards or less), you might want to try a zigzag cutting method. Lay your fabric out on a table. Start cutting your first strip with a pair of scissors along the edge of the fabric, stopping about 2 inches from the end. Do not cut all the way through the end. Move to the other side of the fabric and start making the next cut, for a strip

approximately the same width as the first. Again, stop about 2 inches from the end.

Continue this way until you have worked all across the piece of fabric. The strips will have a zigzag appearance and an awkward look at the ends where you didn't cut all the way through. To ease the turn, simply make tapered cuts at the corners. This will reduce the bulk and help to straighten the fabric.

Tearing strips

Tearing strips with a friend

Using a rotary cutter

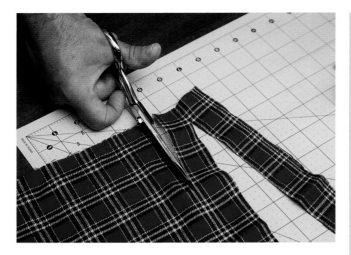

Cutting strips using the zigzag method

Preparing Recycled Fabric

Some people like the idea of recycling old clothes to make rag rugs. If you start cutting apart an old shirt or coat, you will quickly see that the strips produced are short and will require sewing together to get a strip long enough to wind onto a shuttle.

Joining shorter lengths of fabric may seem to be a nuisance, but the overall effect in the woven rug is beautiful. We call these rugs "hit-or-miss" rugs. They had their heyday in the early years of weaving rag rugs because this was the most common way of preparing the rag strips. Back then, rag rug makers were in the mindset of using what they had and would never have gone out and bought new fabric to cut into rags. Though it's common to buy new material for a rag rug today, the traditional hit-or-miss style is still a great way to make a unique and beautiful rug.

If you are going to sew short lengths of rags together, there are two easy ways to do this. For one option, start by overlapping two ends of your strips for about an inch. Then fold them lengthwise. This is a great time to be sure that the wrong side of fabric is turned inside and the pretty side is toward the outside. Using a needle and thread, sew back and forth through the layers to secure them.

Another way to secure the ends is to overlap the ends as before for about an inch and then sew them on a diagonal. This can be done by hand or with a sewing machine. To reduce the bulk, you can cut and remove the free ends.

Shorter lengths can also be joined together without sewing by cutting small slits (about an inch long) on either end of the fabric strip, creating a small hole on each end. Fold the end of the strip back onto itself for about 1 inch, and then cut into the fold for about ½ inch, being careful that you don't cut all the way to the end of the strip. You'll see a hole at the end of your strip when you unfold it.

When you've cut holes in both ends of several strips, you are ready to start joining them together. Start by laying the first piece to your left. Now lay the second strip, coming in from the right, on top of the first strip. Match up the holes or slits.

Hold the join with your left hand and with your right hand bring the other end of the right strip underneath the hole and bring this end up through the hole.

Gently pull on the two strips of fabric to interlock them.

This will make a small bump, but the bumps will add a pleasing texture to the surface of your rug. They can

Overlap the ends of your strips for about an inch, fold them lengthwise with right sides facing out, and then sew back and forth through the layers.

Overlap the ends and sew through the layers on a diagonal, making a seam.

The finished diagonal seam

also cause difficulty in beating the strip down into the rug and create buckles that prevent your rug from lying flat on the floor. To avoid this outcome, be sure that the warp is set wider in the reed. A wider setting such as 6 or 8 ends per inch will produce a larger space for the seam bumps to poke through and allow the rug to lie flat. If you try weaving these strips into a rug warp that has a closer sett of 12–24 ends per inch, you will definitely experience buckling, because the warp threads will have to ride on top of the seam bumps instead of passing to the right or left.

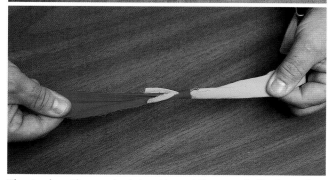

Shorter lengths can be joined by cutting small slits in each end and then interlocking them.

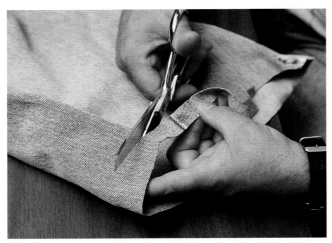
Spiral cuts are a good way to get a long length of fabric from jeans or pants.

It is possible to bypass the sewing with some creative cutting. With a pair of slacks or old blue jeans, you can get long strips by making spiral cuts up the legs of the pants. Start by cutting the legs off the pants up near the crotch, below the back pockets. Now begin to cut around and around the leg on a very slight angle to keep a continuous cut going—the way they cut a spiral ham. You can start at the top or bottom of the leg; it doesn't matter which.

Cut straight through the bulky part of the vertical seam. This may seem very odd, but you are doing fine. These lumps and bumps will add texture to the surface of your rug. Just be sure that your warp is set wide enough in the reed to allow the bumps to surface, as I described before with the interlocked short strips.

Preparing Knit Fabric

Many of us remember making woven pot holders from "loopers" on small square looms in our childhoods. These "loopers" were waste material from factories that made socks—and they are still available today. You can use these sock tops to make rugs, but it is going to take a lot of them to make one rug. Interconnect the loops with each other to make a long strip that can be wound onto a rug shuttle. Because the sock tops are made from a knitted fabric, they are very stretchy. I usually try to avoid knit fabric for this reason; the stretchy fabric makes the rug's width draw in severely, making it difficult to know just how wide the finished rug will be. You can help to avoid this result by pulling on the loops and stretching them out of shape.

You can also make your own giant loopers from old T-shirts. Start by laying the T-shirt onto a flat work

RIGHT SIDE/ WRONG SIDE

One final thing to check before you can start weaving with your rags is whether there is a similar amount of color on both sides of the fabric. As I mentioned in the previous chapter, batik fabrics are wonderful because they look the same on both sides; many other fabrics are printed and have an obvious good side and not-so-good side. This characteristic may not bother you at all because the mix of the two sides can create an attractive look. If the wrong side of the fabric shows up only occasionally, however, it looks like a mistake.

To get a crisp look without any wrong-side mishaps, it is worth taking the time to fold the fabric in thirds and iron the strips. It takes a little while but is truly worth the effort. Starting at one end of a rag strip, fold about a third of the fabric in on itself lengthwise and give a light pressing for about a foot or less. Then fold the other edge in and press it to match. It is a little awkward at first, but you will soon develop a system for doing it quickly. Your finished woven rug will look much neater without the inside of the print showing up on the surface of the rug. ✳

table and straighten it out so it lies flat. With scissors or a rotary cutter and cutting mat, remove the waistband. Now move up approximately ½ inch and cut all the way across the two layers of the shirt to make your first looper.

The side seams remain joined, of course, creating a large loop. Because you have a ½ inch of fabric on each side of the loop, you have now the equivalent of 1 inch total fabric in your loop. Take a moment to admire your loop. Ta-da! Now, I ask you, how great is that?

JOINING LOOPERS

Sock top loopers and T-shirt loopers are joined together the same way. Start by placing a looper to the right of you. Bring a second looper in from the left side and overlap the two loopers so that the edge of the looper on the right is lying on top of the left looper. Now bring the far end of the left looper toward the overlap and loop it up through itself. Pull the loopers away from each other to tighten the knot.

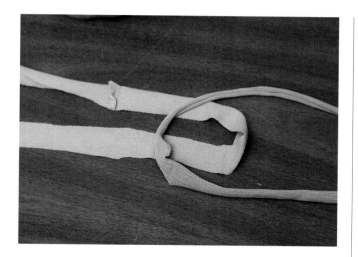

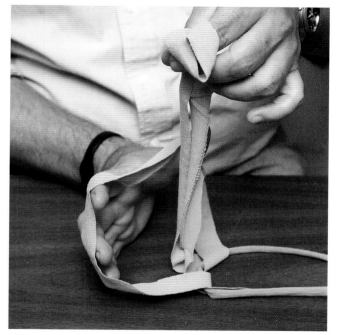

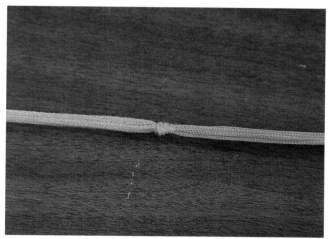

Overlap loopers, and then bring the far end of one looper around the other and back through itself.

The pulling will also stretch the knitted fabric and make it more stable. When you pull the loopers, the raw and cut edges curl inward, making the looper more tubular and round; this is because it is knitted fabric.

WARPING THE LOOM

So you've finished planning out your rug—you've chosen a warp thread and selected and prepared your weft materials. Now it's time to start making the rug, and the first step is warping the loom. To many beginning weavers, the process may seem overwhelming, the terrible, horrible prelude to the much more enjoyable part of weaving. If you think this, maybe you need to be shown how to warp more efficiently, breaking the process down into small, manageable parts. That's what this chapter will show you.

How Much Warp Thread Do You Need?

The first step is to calculate how much warp thread you'll need, and the first part of this calculation is the ends per inch, or epi. This refers to the number of individual threads in your reed. Remember that a rag rug is an unbalanced woven textile—the ratio between the warp threads and the weft material is not the same. (In contrast, the fabric that you just prepared for the rag strips most likely was a balanced weave, having the same number of warp threads and weft threads per inch.) To achieve a thick and heavy rug that's suitable for walking on, we need to get as far away from balanced as possible.

The epi depends on the kind of rug you want to make. A rug is said to be weft faced or weft emphasized when the weft material is the dominant material showing on the surface and the warp threads are buried down into the interior of the rug to give the rug its foundation. For a rug like this, the warp would be spaced rather coarsely in the reed, allowing the weft rags to beat back and cover the warp threads. A rug warp such as this might be set at 6 epi, and the weft rags might be beaten down to 10 or 12 picks or rows per inch.

A warp-faced or warp-emphasized rug is one in which the warp is the dominant factor in the design; to achieve this effect, the warp threads must be crowded together more closely in the reed. A thread that might be set at 12 epi for a balanced weave will now be set at 24 or 36 epi (two to three times closer than for a balanced weave)

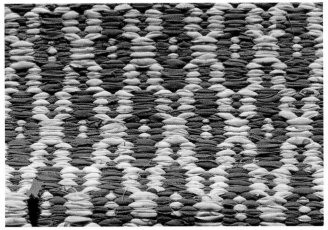

A weft-faced rug

A warp-faced rug

Close-up of an unbalanced weave

to get a warp-faced rug. The weft rows or picks per inch might only be in the neighborhood of 4 or 5.

The examples shown in the photos are clearly unbalanced. Most woven rag rugs fall into an area that is a little unclear, with a setting of 12–16 epi. You could weave with 8/4 cotton thread for both warp and weft at this setting and get a perfectly lovely (balanced) cotton fabric. But in a rag rug the weft material is strips of fabric that are proportionately much larger and heavier, making it an unbalanced weave; with the warp set at 12–16 epi, the weft picks are 4 or 5.

Now to calculate the epi for your rug. Start by taking a ruler and the thread you intend to use as your warp. In this case, we are using 8/4 cotton carpet warp. Wrap the carpet warp firmly around the ruler, placing the threads side by side. If you see the ruler showing through the wraps, you are not getting the threads as close as they need to be—you are trying to calculate the warp as it will be on the loom, under tension. Wrap for 1 inch, and then count the threads; 8/4 cotton will have 24 wraps in a 1-inch space on the ruler, but with a different thread you may get a different figure. Now divide this number in half for Plain Weave or Tabby, or by-two thirds for Twill. This is the standard for calculating all yarns and threads. In our example, 24 divided by 2 for Tabby will give you a setting of 12 epi. For Twill, divide 24 by two-thirds to get 16.

Now let's calculate the total number of ends or warp threads. Simply multiply the epi by the width in the reed. For a rug woven as Tabby and measuring 25 inches wide in the reed, we get 12 epi times 25, or 300 total ends or threads. For a Twill structure, take 16 epi times 25, for a total of 400 total ends or threads.

Next, you need to calculate the warp length. First, think about how long you want the finished rug to be. Then add 20% more to that number for take-up (extra length needed to account for the warp threads going over and under the weft threads instead of straight up the loom). There is quite a lot of take-up when weaving rag rugs because the weft materials are so thick and heavy. When you are weaving conventional fabric, you only need to add 10%. If you are planning on weaving with an extremely heavy weft material, add another 25–30% (i.e., 45–50% total). This is like having insurance to cover the unexpected, especially if you haven't woven a sample first. Some individuals like to weave a sample and calculate exactly what the take-up will be; I tend to add extra right from the beginning and weave by the seat of my pants, knowing that I have that insurance

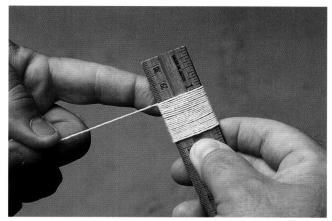
Finding the epi

built in. Next, think about how you are going to finish the rug. Will there be fringe or will you weave a hem? If you are planning on weaving a hem, allow about 3 inches on each end for the woven area of hem; if you are planning on a fringe, then allow about 6 inches extra on each end. Add the finished length, the take-up, and the hem or fringe allowance to get the length you need to weave one rug. If you are planning on weaving several rugs on the same warp, then multiply this number by the number of rugs you are planning on weaving. You're not done yet! The final factor to add in is what is known as loom waste. This is the area of the warp that is used to tie onto the apron rods, front and back, and also the unwoven area from the last weft row of your weaving that continues back and through the reed and harness frames to where you tied onto the back apron rod.

DRAW-IN

This is the perfect time to talk about draw-in. Draw-in is the narrowing of your rug that happens as you weave. Some rag rugs draw in more than others. Weft-face Twill may draw in as much as 10–15%, while a warp-face rug will not draw in at all and might actually measure slightly wider than what it was set in the reed because of the density of the warp.

On average, there is very little draw-in with a conventional rag rug with a sett of 12–16 epi and woven with rags 1–1½ inches wide. If you think that you might experience some draw-in with your rug, be sure to add a little extra to the width in the reed to compensate. ✳

You should usually add between 30 and 36 inches for loom waste, depending on your loom. Add this figure in to your total, and you have the final length for each strand of warp.

Now that you have calculated the warp length, it is time to measure out the warp on either a warping board or a warping mill.

The method I use for warping my loom is known as warping front to back. In this method, you place the measured warp into the reed first and then go to the back of the loom and thread the heddles, tie the warp to the apron rod, wind it onto the warp beam, and finally go the front to tie the warp onto the front apron rod and adjust the tension. Let's break this process down into smaller, easy-to-follow steps.

Winding the Warp

You can wind the warp either on a warping board or on a warping mill. They have exactly the same function: to measure each thread in the warp to the same length. Often, you can wind the entire warp for your rug all at one time. This is because the pegs on the warping board and mill are long and can accommodate the many passes you need to make to measure out the total number of warp threads. Warping boards are inexpensive in comparison to warping mills. If you are handy, you can even make your own warping board. In our example here, I'll show you how to wind the warp using a warping board.

1. Start by making a guide thread in a contrasting color. Measure it to the same length as your desired warp length, and then add a few inches for tying it onto the pegs of the board. This guide thread will outline the path that you are going to take with the actual warp. It is only a guide and not part of the warp.

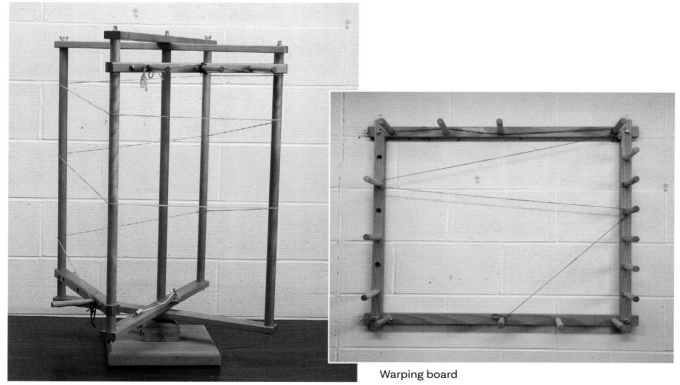

Warping mill

Warping board

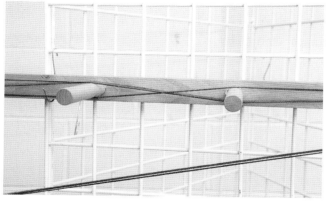

2. Look at the warping board and locate the area where there are three pegs placed rather close together (on the upper left on the warping board shown here). This is the spot where you are going to be winding the warp in a figure eight, and it is referred to as "the cross." The cross helps you keep the threads in a chronological order. This helps you to remember the thread order when placing them in the reed later on.

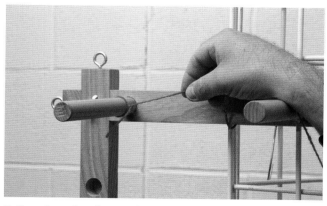

3. Start by tying the guide thread onto the first peg at the beginning of the warping board near the cross.

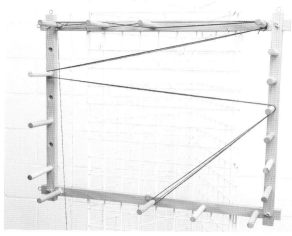

4. Now go to the next peg, passing the guide thread over it; then pass it under the next peg. Now move to the far

right side of the board and go around the top peg. Next, take the thread to the left side of the board and take it around the first peg.

5. Keep moving back and forth between the two sides, going around the next peg down each time, until you come to the end of your guide thread. Tie the guide thread to the nearest peg; any sort of knot will do just fine. Most warping boards are one yard across. This makes it so easy to wind and count, especially if you are measuring your warp in lengths rounded to the nearest yard. This warp in our example is a 3½-yard warp.

TIPS

As you wind the warp:

- Be careful not to wind the warp too tightly. The warp should have a little give and not be as tight as it would be on the loom. If it is too tight, it might bend or break the warping board.
- If you should come to a knot in the warp thread, back up to the nearest end peg, retie the knot, and cut away the excess thread. This will get the knot out of the middle of your warp.
- Count as you go. I use a counting tie that I wrap around and through the warp as I wind it. Place this tie toward the middle of the warp and not at the cross; there will be more than enough ties there later. I like tying in bundles of twenty threads. But that's just me; you can count in any number that makes sense to you. It doesn't really matter as long as you end up with the necessary number of threads. ✳

Tie bundles of warp as you wind in groups of the same number to keep count.

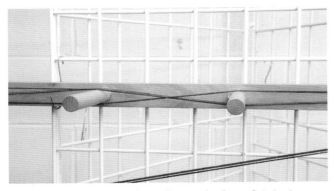

6. Now that the guide thread is on the board, it is time to wind the actual warp. Tie the chosen warp thread to the first peg of the warping board. Take it through the cross, going over and under these next pegs just like you did with the guide thread, and then continue to follow the guide until you reach the last peg and the end of the guide thread. Go around this peg (it doesn't matter whether you go over or under this one). Now follow the path back toward the cross. When you get to the cross, go over the first peg and under the next (the opposite of how you started out), and then out to the peg where you tied on at the beginning. Go around this peg and continue along the same path from beginning peg to the ending peg, following the same route as before.

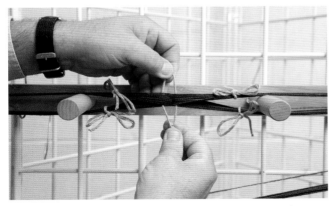

7. When you have the number of threads you need, place a number of ties throughout the warp to secure it and keep it neat. The first tie to make is the cross tie. Locate the cross in the beginning of the warping board and look at the figure eight. With a piece of cord that is thicker than (and a different color from) the warp, go in from the front on one side of the cross, around the back, and back out on the other side to wrap the cord around the center of the cross. Tie a knot at the end of the cord, making a large loop rather than a tight tie. Don't include the guide thread. That will stay on the warping board when you remove the warp later. Now put several more ties throughout the warp.

8. You are now ready to remove the warp from your warping board. Start at the bottom of the warping board and carefully remove the end loop from the peg. Put your hand through the loop, and then grab the warp above the tie that forms the top of the loop and pull it through the loop to make a new loop. Think of your hand like a large crochet hook (and you are chaining with the warp thread).

9. Repeat the process again and again, working your way up the length of the warp and stopping just a few feet from the cross. Pull the cross free from the warping board. Be very careful not to pass the end of the warp through the last loop. This will lock the warp. If you want to secure the warp, simply tie another cord around the entire end, as shown here.

Sleying the Reed

You are now ready to sley the reed. This is the process of putting the warp threads into the reed in their proper and chronological order. We will be using a 12-dent reed.

1. Start by finding two long, flat sticks that will reach from the front beam of the loom to the back beam of the loom. They should extend over the beams just a little so they don't slip and drop off the beams. Lay the reed down on the sticks, which will support the reed as you sley the warp into it.

2. Place the warp's cross on the front beam and undo its chain over the loom's harness frames and back to the back beam of the loom. Wrap the warp around the back beam and tie it tightly to the beam, to prevent the warp from shifting while you work in the front, sleying the reed.

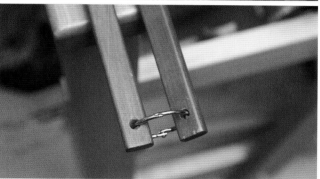

3. From the front of the loom, transfer the cross to a pair of lease sticks. Place a stick on either side of the cross (currently secured by the cord you put there when you made the warp on the warping board). Secure the ends of the lease sticks either with a cord or, my favorite method, with ring binders. Untie the cords that secured the cross in the warp. You do not need them now because the warp is safe on the lease sticks.

4. Slide the lease sticks back toward the castle of the loom and place them on the sticks that hold the reed in place. The lease sticks should now be located between the reed and the castle of the loom. You should have a long length of the warp extending from the lease sticks toward the front of the loom. This is the portion of the warp that you will be sleying into the reed.

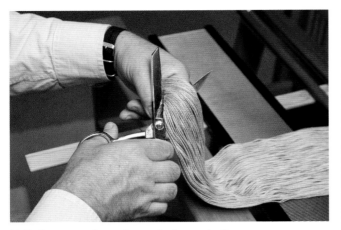

5. Be brave and cut through the end of your warp.

WINDING A SECTIONAL BEAM

If you have a sectional warp beam, you will wind the warp onto it one section at a time. Use a spool rack with a spool of thread for each thread needed per section, and then thread the warp through a tension box. Place the tension box on the back beam of the loom, directly above the section that is to be wound. Attach the warp threads to the warp beam by tying them to the cord that comes up from each section. As you wind the warp, you need to calculate the number of turns needed to achieve the desired length of the warp (based on the circumference of your warp beam). When you have finished winding the section, cut the warp free, secure the ends, and move on to the next section.

Winding the warp sectionally allows you to warp your loom with much more warp than you would be able to do with conventional chain warping. ✳

Sectional warp

6. To get ready to sley the warp, you need to make a few measurements. Start by finding the center of your reed and marking it. Next, find the spot on the reed where you need to start the warp (I am right-handed, so I like to start on the right side of the reed and work across the reed to the left; if you are left-handed, you may prefer to start on the left side of the reed). Lay the tape measure back on the reed and measure half the width of the warp out from the center. Since our warp was wound with 300 total ends and is to be sleyed at 12 epi for 25 inches wide, I need to measure out 12½ inches to the right of the center.

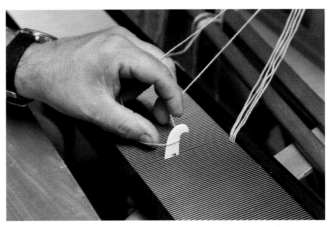

7. Take a sleying hook in your right hand. Bring the hook up from the bottom of the reed. Pull the first warp thread on the right-hand side off the lease sticks, place it in front of the hook, and pull it down through the reed.

8. Work across the reed, sleying it with one thread per dent. When you are finished, you will have the warp centered in the reed (with 12½ inches to the right and left of the center, in our 25-inch example). I like to tie the warp threads that I have sleyed in 1-inch bundles under the reed with a slipknot. That way, if the reed should get bumped and fall off the sticks, your work is saved.

Threading the Heddles

Your next step is to thread the heddles.

1. Untie the warp from the back beam and bring the chain warp forward and over the harnesses to the very front of the loom.

2. Hold the reed in one hand and, with the other, remove the sticks that supported the reed. Flip the reed and place it in the beater of the loom so that the sleyed warp ends are facing toward the castle of the loom and the harnesses. Adjust the warp ends so that there are approximately 12–14 inches of warp coming through the reed. This should be enough warp length to thread through the heddles.

3. Wrap the warp chain around the front beam of the loom and tie it securely. This will prevent the warp threads from shifting and pulling as you thread them through the heddles, keeping them all the same length and helping to prevent tangles in the warp later on.

4. Go to the back of the loom at this point and look at your loom. Is there any way that the loom can be folded up to make getting to the heddles any easier? Some looms have a back beam that is removable. Your loom may also be able to fold up to the castle, allowing you to get very close to the harness frames and heddles. If your loom does have a folding option, be sure to use it. It will make threading easier and save you from having to stretch your arms out for hours at a time. I like to use a low, comfortable stool that lets me sit with the heddles nearly at eye level. If your loom is a Jack-type loom, where the harnesses raise up to make the shed, use a block of wood, a cone of yarn, or a book standing on its end to raise the harnesses up and bring them to your

eye level. Counterbalance and countermarch looms' harness frames are already raised slightly because they are suspended from cords coming down from rollers or jacks at the top of the loom.

5. Untie the first bundle of warp threads, bring them down and under the harness frames, and put them in your left hand.

6. With your right hand, thread the first thread coming out from the reed. You want to take the threads in the same order they were sleyed in. Fold the thread into a small loop and poke it through the heddle eye, being very careful that the thread goes in a straight path through the eye and doesn't get twisted.

7. Thread the heddles according to the threading draft and pattern. After you thread a bundle, be sure to retie it into a slipknot. Continue threading until you have come to the end, and then unfold the loom and reassemble it to its original position. Don't forget to remove the blocks holding up the harness if you are using a Jack-type loom.

Tying the Threads to the Apron Rod

1. Bring the apron rod up and over the top of the back beam. It is very important to have the apron rod and cords going over the back beam because the warp needs to travel over the back beam and then down to the warp beam. This will keep the warp threads on a straight and horizontal plane, resulting in a good clear shed when you are weaving. Adjust the apron cord length so that you can tie onto the apron rod.

2. Untie the first bundle of threaded warps on the right-hand side and take them over the apron rod. Split them in half and bring one half up and around on the right and the other half up and around on the left of the bundle. Tie the two ends together with a square knot.

3. Now go to the left side and do the same with the bundle on the far left. This will support the apron rod as you tie the rest of the warp to the rod.

4. Tie the rest of the warp threads onto the apron rod.

Winding the Warp onto the Warp Beam

1. Before you start to wind the warp onto the warp beam, you must remember to go to the front of the loom and untie the warp from the front beam. After you do this, you will want to use your hands and straighten out the warp to check for tangles.

2. Bring the beater forward and rest it against the front beam.

3. Go to the side of the loom and step on the brake treadle to release the tension on the brake cable. Locate the crank that moves the warp beam and turn it clockwise. This will wind the warp forward and onto the warp beam.

4. If the beater moves forward and rests against the castle of the loom, stop and untangle the warp, or you risk tearing warp threads.

5. As you wind the warp onto the warp beam, be sure to separate the layers of warp by using sticks, heavy paper, or (my favorite) single-face corrugated cardboard. This will help to maintain an even tension on the warp.

6. Stop after every couple of turns and pull on the warp chain in the front of the loom. This will help you keep a tight warp and prevent the cardboard from slipping. If you have a friend hold onto the warp as you wind it, that can be helpful too—but you can certainly do this task all by yourself. Wind the warp until the end of the warp chain is at the front beam and then stop.

Tying onto the Front Apron Rod

1. Locate the take-up mechanism on the cloth beam. This is usually on the right side and is called the ratchet and pawl. Release it so the cloth beam will turn and allow the apron rod to come up over the front beam and stop just beyond the beam.

2. Cut through the end of the warp. You can do this by cutting through the loop ends with your scissors or by simply cutting straight across the end.

3. You will now have hundreds of individual ends that need to be secured. Tie them in large bundles or take the time to count out each inch's worth of warp and tie these in individual bundles using a slipknot.

4. Starting on either the right or the left, begin tying the warp to the apron rod, an inch's worth of warp threads at a time. Take them over the apron rod and down around the bar, and then split the bundle into two equal parts and bring them back up around the outside of the original bundle. Tie the first part of a square knot with the two small bundles.

5. Now move to the opposite side of the warp and repeat step 4 with the first inch's worth of warp threads on that side.

6. Continue going back and forth from side to side, tying one-inch bundles of warp to the apron rod, only securing each bundle with the first half of a square knot.

7. When you reach the middle and tie the last half square knot, pull up on it firmly and then tie the second portion of the square knot to complete it. Feel the tension of the knot. This is what you want the rest of the knots to feel like.

8. Working from side to side again, complete the other knots, pulling up on them and bringing them to the same tension as the center knot before tying them off.

As I tie the second half of each square knot, I take the tails of warp thread and poke them down on the side of the knot to help myself keep track of which knots are completed.

9. When you have finished tying the knots, take a moment and gently press down on the warp threads to feel whether the tension seems even. If not, go back and redo the knots that need to be adjusted.

10. When every knot feels the same, you may want to add additional tension to the warp before you start to weave. Use the ratchet and pawl to tighten the warp. Don't make it too tight, though, or you won't be able to get a shed when you step on the treadle. If the warp is too tight, readjust your tension by taking the pawl back one notch or by gently depressing the brake assembly.

11. If you haven't tied up the treadles until now, this is a good time to do it so you can check the shed. Many four-harness looms have six treadles. This allows you to have two Tabby treadles and four Twill treadles. The tie-up arrangement can be any way you like. Some weavers will place the Tabby treadles on the far outside and tie the four Twill treadles in the middle; others tie the Twill treadles on the left-hand side and the last two treadles to weave Tabby. Any way that pleases you will work. The Tabby treadles are tied up as follows: One treadle should be tied to lift harnesses 1 and 3, and the second Tabby treadle should lift harnesses 2 and 4. This allows you to alternate the odd-numbered harnesses against the even-numbered harnesses. The four Twill treadles should be tied to lift harnesses 1 and 2, 2 and 3, 3 and 4, and 1 and 4, respectively.

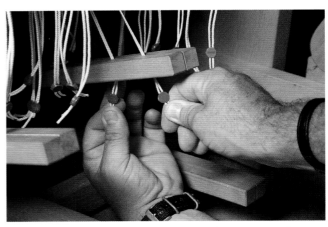

When this job is done, you are ready to step on the treadles to see whether you have a clear shed (if not, adjust the warp tension, as described in step 10).

Congratulations! You have warped your loom and are ready to weave. Now that wasn't so bad, was it?

WEAVING A RAG RUG

You are now ready to start weaving your rug! Well, you are almost ready. Take a look at where the warp ends are tied to the apron rod. The knots force the warp ends into a lot of little V formations. This is the way it's supposed to be, but it's not a great way to start off your weaving—you want the warp to be spaced evenly in your rug, and it's not right now. To even out the warp, you'll weave some waste material (maybe some cheap old yarn) into the warp for about an inch or more in Plain Weave. This evens out the warp and creates a firm base to start your rug from. This waste material will be cut out after the rug is woven, when you begin to do the finishing.

Ah! The finishing is something you need to think about right now. Do you want to have fringe on your rug, or will you simply roll a hem on each end? Fringes look beautiful and are the expected finish for a rug, but a rolled hem makes washing the rug much easier because fringes get tangled in the wash. In the next chapter, we will talk more about how to finish your rug, but the reason we are having all this talk about finishes now is that the way you plan to finish your rug makes a big difference in where you place the waste material at the beginning. If you are planning on doing a rolled hem, you can start weaving the waste material just above the knots where you tied the warp to the apron rod (leave about an inch or so above the knots for a little ease). If you are planning on a fringe, start weaving in the waste material about three inches above the knots. After you finish weaving the rug, when you remove it from the loom, you will untie the knots on the front apron rod. This length of the warp is going to be the fringe on this end. The remaining unwoven warp that makes up the loom waste at the other end will be for the fringe on the other end.

Before you start weaving in the waste material, check the tension of the warp. The tension that was put on the warp by tying it to the apron rod is usually not enough. The warp should be firm to the touch when you press down on it with an open hand. If you are weaving on a counterbalance or countermarch loom, you can put even more tension on the warp because the warp threads will be moving in both directions, up and down, when you step on a treadle to make the shed. If you are using a jack loom, the warp should be slightly looser because the warp threads only move up when the shed is being made. If the warp is too tight, you compromise the shed and it may be difficult to get a wide enough shed to get a shuttle through.

A temple will help to keep the width of your rug more uniform.

Weave the Waste Material

Weave the waste material with a Tabby treadling. Weave the first row with the 1 and 3 Tabby pick and the second row with the opposite 2 and 4 pick. Then beat the two picks together. By not beating after each Tabby pick, you close the gap much faster. Weave a few more picks the same way for an inch or so to make this firm foundation. Don't be concerned with how this section looks; remember that this is only the waste material.

If you are planning on using a temple (a stretcher that helps to maintain the width of your rug as you weave), you should place it on the waste now.

Weave the Heading

You are now ready to start weaving the heading for your rug. The heading is one of the most important parts of the rug because it provides a stable beginning and ending for your rug and prevents the rags from coming undone. On many commercially woven rag rugs that you find for sale in discount stores, the knots are tied directly up against the rags. This is poor construction: If for some reason the knots become untied, the rags will slip free and the rug will come apart. A heading eliminates this problem. If you want a rolled hem on your rug, you should allow several inches of heading so that you can roll the hem twice and stitch it in place. If you are planning on a fringed edge, weave only about ½ inch of heading at the beginning and at the end of your rug. At the beginning and end of the heading, take the ends of your weft around the last warp end and lay them back into the first and last picks of the heading.

To prevent excess draw-in and later buckling in your rug, make an easy transition from the heading to the first pick of your rag weft. There is too much difference in size between a single strand of 8/4 cotton warp and a rag weft, so I use two strands of 8/4 cotton carpet warp wound together on a bobbin as the weft material for my headings.

In addition, I weave the heading material into the warp with a deliberate arch in the middle to introduce more of the weft material into the warp; this also helps with the draw-in.

If I'm going to be finishing a rug with a rolled hem, I weave the heading in one of two ways. The first is to weave the hem area in a simple Tabby weave. The second method of weaving hem areas is something I

Weave the heading with an arch in the middle.

Notice the places where the weft is doubled back into the same shed to create a fold line for the hem.

Wind your rags tightly onto the shuttle, and without too much overflow.

adapted from instructions I found for weaving hems on dish towels and placemats. Look at the weaving in the photo above. You will see that there are places where the weft is doubled back into the same shed. This creates a double row and makes an obvious fold line. To make the double fold line, simply take your shuttle around the last warp thread to lock it in place—or, if you are using a floating selvedge, go around it—and then throw the shuttle back into the same shed. The two doubled lines will make it much easier to see where to fold the hem and to get straight lines. Also notice that the doubled rows are not evenly spaced: The area closest to the rug is wider than the area near the waste material. This helps to avoid extra buildup under the fold.

Weave with Rags

When you have finished weaving the beginning heading for your rug, you are ready to weave your first row of rags. Wind your rags onto a rug shuttle tightly, so as to wind on as much material as you can without the shuttle getting too bulky. If the shuttle is overwound and bulging at the sides, you are going to have a difficult time getting it to pass smoothly through the open shed.

Make a 5- to 6-inch taper at the end of your rag strip with a pair of sharp scissors.

Following your treadling instructions, weave the first pick of rags across the warp, leaving approximately half the tapered end sticking out from the edge. Beat the rags into place. Open the same shed again and now wrap the tapered end back into the shed and beat again. This will make a good-looking beginning selvedge, without a bulky buildup or a raw bit of rag hanging out.

Use scissors to taper the ends of your rag strips.

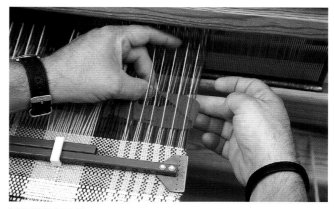

Tapered strips will make a less bulky selvedge.

Continue to weave the rags into your rug, following the treadling instructions. Here are some things to keep in mind as you go along:

- Make sure to angle the weft or arch the weft in the middle to prevent excess draw-in.
- You also want to make sure you beat the rags firmly into place. I beat with an open shed first and then change to the next shed and beat again. This helps to pack the rags firmly into place and creates a tight rug that will wear well.
- If you are using a temple to help with the draw-in, be sure to move the temple forward every 1½ to 2 inches as you weave. Always move the temple first before you advance your warp. This will prevent any chance of the temple's sharp teeth being dragged across the front breast beam and scratching it.
- Advance the warp frequently. This will go without saying as you start to weave. Rags weave up quickly, and you may get between 4 and 5 weft picks to the inch. After 3–4 inches of weaving, you will notice that the shed is getting smaller and it is harder to get the shuttle through; advancing the warp will make the shed much wider again.
- Be mindful of how your selvedge edge looks. The edge of your rug will never be as neat or clean-edged as that of a dish towel or, for that matter, the fabric that you just bought and cut up to make this rug—it's simply impossible. Your weft is heavy cut strips of fabric, not thread, so it cannot make as smooth a selvedge edge. You can make the edge as smooth as possible, however, by using your fingers to place the bent strip neatly at each edge.
- When you get to the end of the shuttle's rags, it will be time to add a new shuttle. Cut the ends on a long taper, and it will be easy to overlap the tapers and get a nice, neat splice.
- Measure as you go so that you can keep track of how much you have woven. You can do this several ways. You can pin a tape measure to the beginning of your rug at the selvedge edge and just keep pinning it to the rug's woven surface as you go. You can also just measure as you weave and stick a pin in at the edge every foot or so, keeping track of how much you have woven.
- This brings up the point of how much to weave. Remember that the warp on the loom is under tension. When the rug is removed from the loom, it will relax and tighten up, getting shorter. On average, I weave 14 inches on the loom for each 12

inches of finished rug I want. So a rug that needs to be 60 inches finished will be woven 70 inches long on the loom. Of course, there are always exceptions. Always, always, always allow yourself to be open to the fact that the rug might not come out exactly to the measurement that you want it to be. It is a rag rug, after all, and not a quilt patch that needs to fit precisely. If the rug doesn't fit the way you want it to in the place where you thought it should go, you can find another place for it. Sometimes I warp the loom with the whole intention of just weaving up the rags I have on hand: when the rags run out, the rug is done. Or I weave until I come to the end of my warp, regardless of how many rags I have left to weave. I can always add them to my stash and use them in another rug sometime. There are far greater things to worry about than the exact measurement of a rag rug. Live freely and weave happy!

Weave the Other Heading and Waste

When you get to the end of your rug, finish it in the same manner in which you started it. Let the rag weft extend out from the selvedge edge about 5 inches and cut it off. Then open the shed and back the rag out a little bit so that you can cut it at a taper. Once the end is tapered, wrap the end around the last warp end and put it back into the shed, using just your fingers to manipulate it into place.

When you are pleased with the way the selvedge looks, beat the weft again to lock it into place. Next, weave the ending heading so it matches the beginning heading.

Hold on! You are not ready to take the rug off the loom just yet. Finish by weaving some waste material right up next to the final heading. This way, when the rug is cut free from the loom and untied from the front apron rod, it is in a stable condition. You could leave it just the way it is for a long time without the fear of the headings unraveling.

Remove Rug from Loom

There are two ways you can remove the rug from the loom. If you have warped your loom for just the one rug, then you can safely cut the warp behind the harness frames. Doing so will give you about 12–14 inches of warp extending out beyond the final waste material that

Tie slipknots to hold the warp ends after you cut them.

you can use for the fringe of your rug. When you untie the knots in the front, that warp length will be the fringe for the other side of the rug. If you have planned on a hem and no fringe is wanted, then you can cut the warp somewhere between the waste material and the reed. At the other end, you will cut the warp ends between the knots and the waste material section.

But perhaps you have warped your loom for several rugs and want to take this one off the loom right now and finish it. In this case, you want to be careful not to lose the ends of warp from the reed and harnesses as you remove the rug from the loom. Advance the warp so that the heading and waste material are over the warp beam, plus enough warp length for a fringe if that's how you're finishing it.

Relax the tension on the warp. This will help prevent the warp ends from flying back through the reed as you cut them. I like to count and cut the warp ends in 1-inch sections; as I cut the ends, I immediately tie them into

slipknots. This prevents them from slipping through the dents in the reed. Work your way across the warp, counting threads, cutting them, and tying them into slipknots.

Then untie the knots at the front of the loom and remove the rug.

When you are all finished, take a moment to look at your new rug for the first time. Put it on the floor and admire it the way it's intended to be admired. Until now, you have been looking at your rug from between waist height and eye level for all the time that you have been weaving. Now you can see your rug from standing height. Doesn't it look different? All of a sudden, the selvedge edges are much more acceptable, at five feet or more away from your eye. Clap your hands together and do the Happy Weaver Dance. (But not on your rug just yet, because, you see, you haven't hemmed the rug or tied fringes so far.) Congratulations on a rug well woven!

FINISHING YOUR RUG

I think of finishing a rug as a two-part endeavor. The first part protects the weft, and the second part protects the warp. Your first encounter with weft protection started with the waste material that you wove into the warp at the beginning of your weaving to spread the warp ends into their proper and uniform spacing. The waste material that you wove in at the very end next to the ending heading is also a weft protector. At both ends, the waste material keeps the heading from becoming unwoven when the rug is off the loom. Of course, the waste material must eventually come out and be replaced by something else that will protect the header. This is where your finishing choice comes in.

Finishing with a Rolled Hem

If you decide to roll a hem, you have made an excellent choice. It's fast and easy to do, and you will never have to worry about the fringes tangling or disintegrating from repeated washings. To roll a hem, you will need approximately 2½–3 inches of woven heading so that you have enough to fold the heading fabric twice. This will put the cut and raw edge into the interior of the hem and protect it from fraying. While we're talking about fraying, before I cut the waste material from the hem area, I squeeze a bead of Fray Check on the area between the waste material and the hem and let it dry for a few minutes.

1. Cut the waste material off with a sharp pair of scissors.

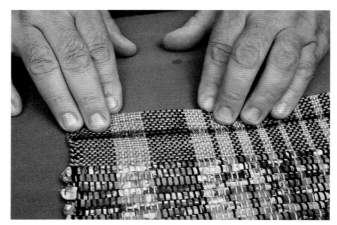

2. Begin folding the hem, using a hot steam iron to help press down the folds. If you wove double lines into your heading, start by folding the cut edge up to the second double line closest to the rug.

3. Carefully press the fold with the steam iron. Then fold the hem again, placing the first doubled row right up against the edge of the rags, and press again. Use T-pins or Wonder Clips to hold the hem in place.

4. Next, with a tapestry needle and strong thread, sew the edge of the hem down. To be sure you have enough thread to go across the rug, measure out about twice the width of the rug. With your threaded needle, go behind the first warp thread and then into the fold of the hem fabric.

5. Pull the thread through, leaving 6 inches of the thread hanging out at the end. Go back up and catch the next warp end, and then go back down into the hem and pull tightly.

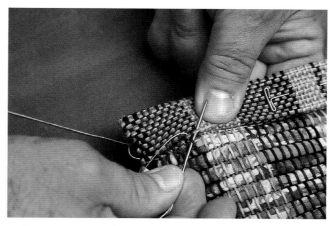

6. Continue to work across the rug in this way, securing the hem. Remove the T-pins or clips as you go to make the sewing easier.

7. When you get to the end of your rug, close up the hem's edge with a simple overcast stitch.

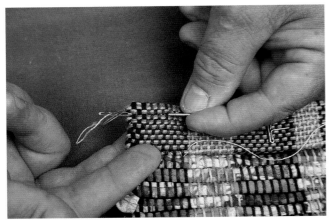

8. Then take the needle and push it into the hem for about 2 inches before bringing it out, to bury the end of the thread in the interior of the hem.

9. Trim the thread up close to the hem. Close up the other end in the same way with the 6-inch tail you left at the beginning.

Finishing with a Fringe

If you want to give your rug a fringed edge, then you will start by laying it on a table, with the edge of the rug and the waste material right at the table's edge. Place something heavy on the rug to keep it from sliding around as you work. You can use an old cast-iron pan or similar heavy object, or you can hold the rug down with a board and two C-clamps. With the rug in place at the table's edge, lay the board on top of the rug. The board needs to be a few inches longer than the rug is wide so that it can extend beyond the rug's selvedge and make a place to attach the C-clamps. Put the C-clamps on each end of the board (you can protect the underside of the table with a piece of folded cardboard) and tighten them down until the rug cannot move.

You are now ready to start tying overhand knots along the edge of your rug. I am right-handed, so the photos that illustrate this process will all be working from right to left, but you can accomplish the same task moving from left to right if this is a more comfortable orientation for you.

1a. Start by carefully snipping the loops in the selvedge of the waste material. This will make removing the waste material much easier. Do not remove all the waste material right away. You are going to take it out a little at a time. If you pull it all out right away, you will have nothing there to hold the heading in as you work.

1b. Let's take a moment to think about the size of the knots. If there are too many warp ends in the knot, then it becomes bulky and the finished edge of the rug looks out of proportion to the rest of the rug. I use approximately half an inch of warp threads per knot. I try to always have an even number of warp ends making up the knot. It would be nice if all the knots had the same number of ends in them, but because of the design of the rug, it doesn't always work out this way. You might have a few knots with more or fewer warp ends in them. Oh, well, that's just the way it works out sometimes— and no one will notice when the rug is on the floor. If you have used floating selvedges in the rug, include them into the first and last knots.

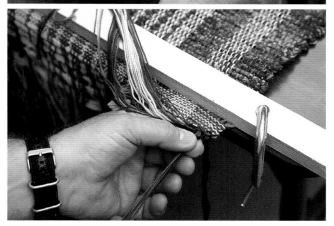

2a. The most commonly used knot for fringes is an overhand knot. There are two ways to go about making these knots. The first is to simply count out the next group of threads, removing the waste material from them; make a large loop with the threads, pull the tails through the loop, slide the loop up close to the rug's edge, and tighten the knot by pulling on the tails of the warp ends.

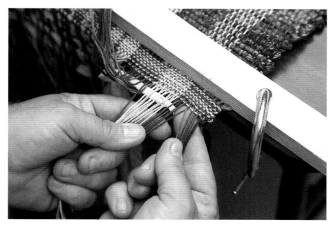

2b. A second variation that I like a little better is to exchange the last warp thread from each group of threads with the first warp thread from the next group of threads. The crossing of these two ends helps to close the gap between the knots.

3a. When you have finished tying the knots on both ends of your rag rug, it's time to trim the fringe. The length of the fringe is a matter of personal choice. I prefer to have a fringe that's about 3–4 inches long. This is short enough that the fringe rarely gets tangled; it is also easy to shake out or comb the fringe so it looks nice and neat on the floor. To cut the fringe to an even length, you can lay the rag rug on a table with the knotted edge 3–4 inches from the table's edge. Then, with a sharp pair of scissors, cut the fringe nice and straight.

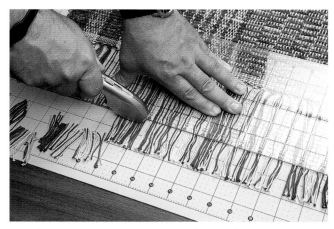

3b. If you have a rotary cutter with a guide and a self-healing mat, you can use them to easily cut a nice, straight fringe. Lay the rug on the mat, lining up the edge of the rug with the mat's grid. Straighten out the rug's fringe with a comb or hairbrush. Then lay the clear plastic guide on the fringe and line it up along the length where you want to make your cut. Apply a little pressure on the guide so it doesn't shift, and use the rotary cutter to cut along the guide, moving away from you. Then turn the rug around and do the other side.

There now! Your fringed rug is finished and ready to put on the floor and enjoy for years to come.

Finishing with a Damascus Edge

Another way of securing your heading's weft is to do a Damascus edge. You sometimes find this edge on Oriental rugs. Damascus is in the Middle East, after all, so the name makes perfect sense. All that trivia aside, this style of finishing makes for a tight, strong edge that is decorative as well. It's also a lot of fun to do.

Pull down on the second warp thread gently with your left hand. (This will be easy to do if you have the rug secured on the table with a heavy weight or the board and C-clamps.) Now pull up (toward the main body of the rug) on the active thread to tighten your knot. This is a half hitch knot.

1. A Damascus edge is nothing more than a series of half hitches. Start by removing the waste material from a small section of warp threads. Working from the right side, take the first warp thread on the right and place it on top of the next warp thread to its left. We will refer to this first thread as the active thread because it is the one that is moving. Take the end of the active thread behind the second thread and bring it up through the loop that was created.

2. Now repeat the process again, with the second warp thread becoming the new active thread and moving over and around the next thread to its left. Tie the knot in the same way as before and pull up tight. Continue this way all the way across the rug to the last warp end. Since there isn't another thread for this last thread to go around, we will just ignore it.

3. Take a look at the edge of your rug. You will notice that there is a braid on the bottom side of the rug's edge and all the warp ends with the exception of the last end are lying on top of the rug. The edge that you have just done is known as a half Damascus edge. To complete the edge treatment and make it a full Damascus edge, turn the rug over and start again on the (new) right-hand side and repeat the whole process over again. The warp end that you couldn't use at the end on the first side will now be the first active thread on the second side.

4. When you have completed both sides of your rug, you will have a braided edge on both sides of the heading, with the warp threads coming out of the center of the braided edge. At this point you can trim the fringe as you would for an ordinary fringed rug (or twist or braid the fringe, as described below).

The Damascus edge is a slow process, but it is a lot of fun to do. It results in a secure edge, with no need to fear that the heading will come out; it is also very pretty to look at. Because it is slow to do, you will not find this type of finishing on a rug for a commercial market. Do it for yourself or for a very special friend who will appreciate your efforts.

The Other Side of Finishing: Protecting the Warp

Up to this point, we have been talking about protecting the weft of your rug. Now I would like to address the idea of protecting the warp threads from disintegrating from the wear of walking and washing. Please do not panic, thinking your rug's beautiful fringe is going to fall apart right away. It won't, especially if you have used a cotton-polyester blend thread for your warp, but you can protect your fringe further by doing some additional finishing on it.

THREE-STRAND BRAID

I will sometimes make a three-strand braid with my fringe. Divide the fringe into bundles and then make a braid from each bundle the same way you would braid someone's hair. Braiding takes up some of the threads' length, so take this into account and add in a little extra length when you trim the fringe. Braid the fringe to the desired length and then make an overhand knot on the end of the braid to keep it from coming undone. Braiding takes a great amount of time to do. I once timed myself and found it took me twice as long to finish the rug as it did to warp and weave it.

Braided warp fringe

TWISTED FRINGE

My all-time favorite way of finishing the fringe is to do a twisted fringe. I start by cutting my entire fringe to the same length, about 20% longer than I want my finished fringe to be. This will allow for the take-up that results from the twisting. The twist that builds up in the fringe will secure the edge of the heading, making it unnecessary to tie knots up against the heading first when doing a twisted fringe. If you have already tied knots or done a Damascus edge, however, that's perfectly fine. It's just more security. Sometimes we switch directions in our thinking and decide to put a twisted fringe on our rug after tying all those knots. That is perfectly all right. It's good looking, it's secure, and your rug is just the way you want it to look, right? Right!

 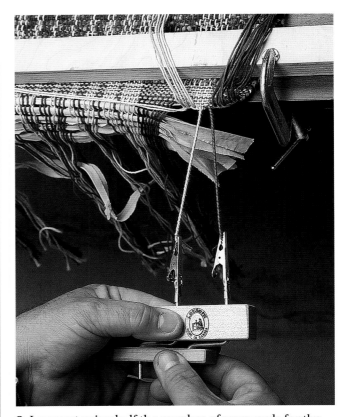

1. To make a twisted fringe, take two groups of threads and twist them in the same direction to build up tension and then let the groups twist back on each other in the opposite direction. You can do this by hand, but it is much faster and easier to do with a fringe twister. A fringe twister is made up of several alligator clips soldered onto some heavy wire and two blocks of wood that make up the body and handle.

2. I suggest using half the number of warp ends for the twisted fringe as you had for the epi. If your warp was set at 12 epi, then use six ends of warp for the twisted fringe. When forming my groups, I cross the warp ends (as when tying knots for a fringe) to prevent gaps between the groups of twisted fringe. Place three warp ends in the teeth of one of the alligator clips and the other three warp ends in the teeth of the other alligator clip. Gently pull on the fringe twister to see whether the groups need to be adjusted to make them even at the ends. Now hold the body of the twister in your left hand and with your right hand turn the handle to the right several times so you can see the twist building up. Count how many turns you are putting into your fringe. You want to turn it until the fringe seems to be noticeably overtwisted. You need this much twist in the fringe so it can balance itself out in the end. A 7-inch length of precut fringe may need 25–30 turns of the twister to create enough twist. Relax the fringe twister just a little and see the two groups of warp kink up a little.

3. You are now ready to let the bundles twist back on themselves. This is so easy to do. Simply let the fringe twister fall down off the edge of the table. It will act like a counterweight and the fringe will automatically twist in the opposite direction.

4. After the fringe twister has slowed down and relaxed, undo the ends from the clips and immediately tie an overhand knot on the end of the twisted strand to secure it.

5. Repeat this all across the rug's edge. If your knots at the end are not all aligned perfectly, that is quite all right. Don't worry about it. As a matter of fact, one time I made all the knots fall at the exact same place and the knots crowded each other out, making the fringe splay outward. I had to redo the fringe by undoing every other knot and making them slightly higher or lower than the knots on either side.

After Finishing

As you can see, there are a number of different ways to finish a rag rug. Some are more elaborate than others, and some take more time to complete. In any of these cases, the whole idea is to make a finish that is appropriate for your rug and that will not only look good but also give your rug years on the floor for you to enjoy.

If, after you have finished your rug and put it on the floor, you notice that there are waves and wrinkles in it, you can get rid of the waves by pressing the rug with a steam iron. Lay your rug on a firm surface like the floor. Place a damp towel on top of the rug and press it with a very hot steam iron. You could also take it to a cleaner, where they can put it on a large steaming press such as the type they might use to press slacks. For a small amount of money, your cleaner will do an exceptional job.

When considering the perfect place on the floor for the rag rug, be mindful of the flooring that it is going to be resting on. Tile and polished hardwood floors are slippery and may present a hazard for the people stepping on the rug. You don't want the rug to slide out from under someone and cause them to fall. Try placing a rubber mat under the rag rug to help it stay in place. You can purchase these mats at many stores that sell carpeting and Oriental rugs or in many large national chain stores in their kitchen and bath areas. These mats look a lot like rubber-coated netting and are sometimes used for kitchen shelf liners.

Your rag rugs can take a lot of abuse, from being stepped on to frequent vacuuming. You can even take the rugs outside and hang them over a wash line or balcony railing and beat them with a broom or old-time carpet beater. When it comes down to washing them, don't be afraid to put them into the washing machine for a good wash to get rid of any ground-in dirt or little gifts left behind by your pets. If your rug is too large to fit into the washing machine, you can put it into the bathtub with 2 or 3 inches of warm soapy water and give it a good scrubbing with a nylon-bristle vegetable brush (like you might use to clean dirt off of potatoes). You could also put the rug over a picnic table or on a wooden deck and scrub it there. Just be sure to rinse it to get rid of all the excess soap from the wash water and then hang the rug out to dry. You can dry rugs in a dryer, but I prefer to hang them outside on a sunny day.

WITH HEARTFELT THANKS

This is my second book about weaving rag rugs. When my editor, Candi Derr, asked me to consider writing a second book on rag rugs with a focus on using recycled materials, I jumped on the idea. After all, that was the original idea in the first place. Rag rugs in the past were woven from old and worn fabrics that had outgrown their usefulness. As you page through this book, you will see Candi's and my vision to use all kinds of fabrics that may otherwise have been tossed in the trash: plastic bags, ripped and torn quilts, and moth-eaten blankets, as well as mouse-eaten flannel fabrics. Candi, this was so much fun, and I thank you for your idea. It's always a pleasure to work with you and our publisher, Stackpole Books.

Thank you, Kathy Eckhaus, my genius photographer, who knows just how to translate into images what I am trying to say in words. Kathy can envision what readers need to see before they tackle a project. You might ask, "How does Kathy know how to do that?" Kathy is a weaver herself.

Lastly, I am forever grateful to my patient, loving wife, Bink, who has helped my every step of the way. Bink stayed with me and guided me through a pandemic and house move and kept me on track. She has been my proofreader, rug finisher, and weaver from time to time. When my mind goes spinning out in left field, Bink reels me in. Thank you, honey, for all your help. I love you.

A special thanks must also go out to all of you, my readers who have used my other books and given me valuable feedback. Thank you.

Photographer Kathy Eckhaus getting the perfect rug shot.

VISUAL INDEX

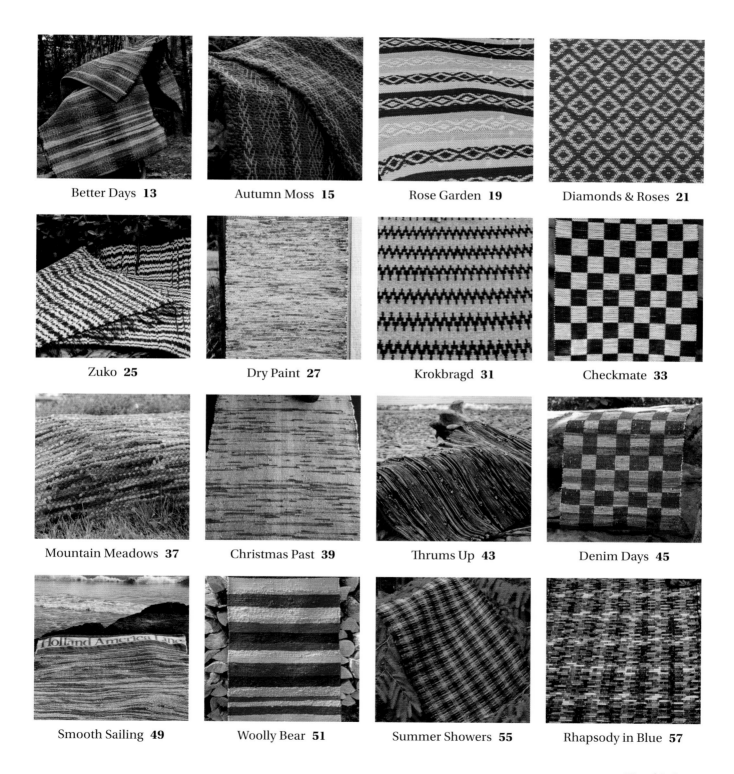

Better Days **13**

Autumn Moss **15**

Rose Garden **19**

Diamonds & Roses **21**

Zuko **25**

Dry Paint **27**

Krokbragd **31**

Checkmate **33**

Mountain Meadows **37**

Christmas Past **39**

Thrums Up **43**

Denim Days **45**

Smooth Sailing **49**

Woolly Bear **51**

Summer Showers **55**

Rhapsody in Blue **57**

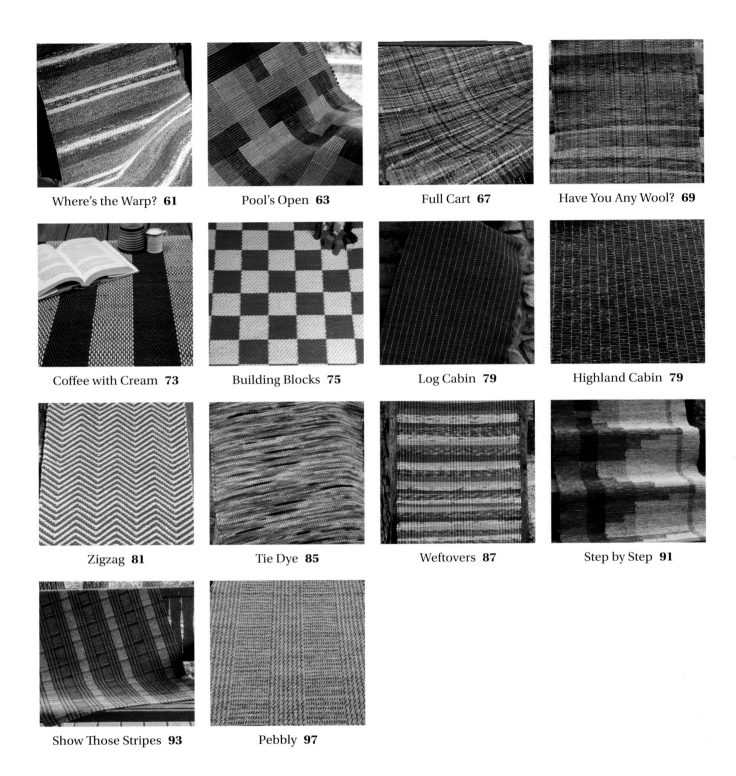